A Book of
Feasts and Seasons

For my mother and father with thanks

A Book of Feasts and Seasons

Joanna Bogle

First published in 1986
Reprinted 1988, 1990

This new edition published in 1992
Reprinted 1995, 1996, 1998, 2002, 2006

Gracewing
2 Southern Avenue, Leominster
Herefordshire HR6 0QF

ISBN 0 85244 217 3

Typeset by Action Publishing Technology Ltd,
Gloucester, GL1 5SR

Acknowledgements

Acknowledgements and thanks are given to Longman Group Ltd., for permission to use extracts from *Pilgrims England* by William Purcell; to Blackie and Sons for the extracts from the *Flower Fairies* poems and from *A Little Book of Old Rhymes;* to Hawthorn Press for the extracts about celebrating Whitsun from *Festivals, Family, and Food;* to Associated Book Publishers (UK) Ltd., and to Methuen Children's Books for the section on Christmas in pioneer America from Laura Ingalls Wilder's *Little House on the Prairie;* to Mayhew McCrimmon for Luke Connaughton's *Love is His Way;* to Faber and Faber for the extracts from Alison Uttley's *A Country Child;* to Rabbi Lionel Blue for his vegetable pie recipe; to the Oxford University Press for the information on nursery rhymes from Iona and Peter Opie's *Oxford Dictionary of Nursery Rhymes;* to Bell and Hyman for the extracts from Christina Hole's *Easter and its Customs;* to Dover publications, New York, for the extract from *Christmas Customs and Traditions;* to David and Charles for the extracts from Margaret Baker's *Folklore and Customs of Rural England;* to The Wanderer newspaper, USA, for the *Blessing of a Christmas Tree* and for the section on *St Wenceslaus;* to Father Mark Elvins for quotes from his *Old Catholic England* published by the Catholic Truth Society; to Anthony Cooney for his piece on St George, originally written for the *Roman Chronicle,* published by the Catholic Printing Company of Farnworth; to Penguin Books for the extract on St Thomas a Becket from Donald Attwater's *Penguin Dictionary of Saints;* to *The Times* for the letter about the 1914 Christmas truce; to Burns and Oates for *Hail, glorious Saint Patrick* and *O great Saint David;* to Messrs Darton, Longman and Todd for the extracts from the Jerusalem Bible, published and Copyright 1966, 1967, and 1968 by Darton, Longman and Todd Ltd., and Doubleday and Co. Inc., and used by permission of the publishers; to Stephen Holmes for his piece on St Rule and St Andrew; to A.P. Watt Ltd., for two prayers from the *Divine Office,* for St Blaise's Day and St Stephen's Day; to the *Yorkshire Evening Post* for the news item about the alleged apparition in 1875; to Pat Kennison for the recipes for Australian Christmas pudding and for ginger log; to my mother-in-law Susan Bogle for the recipe for crystallised fruit peel; and to Wim Peeters of Amersfoort and his family, for items on

Acknowledgments

St Nicholas and Holy Innocents. I am particularly indebted to J. Alan Smith, editor of "Prag", whose Ascension hymn I reproduce in this book: he wrote the hymn deliberately to the tune of "Will ye no come back again" as a way of honouring the memory of "Bonnie Prince Charlie", for whom that song was sung by loyal Jacobites after Culloden. Mr Smith also found me the lovely hymn for St Alban's Day. For the information on the traditions of the turkey, I am indebted to an article in *Asian Affairs* (Journal of the Royal Central Asian Society) vol 57, 1970, by Olaf Caroe. This was drawn to my attention by George Chowdharay-Best, who also gave me other useful information on the subject. For the roast lamb recipes (Easter Sunday) I thank the New Zealand Meat Producers Board, & recommend their excellent "New Zealand Lamb International Cookbook."

Great efforts have been made to check the copyright of all material quoted. One or two items proved impossible to trace, despite extensive library research—if copyright has been infringed I am sincerely sorry and will rectify the matter in future editions.

A Note about Measurements

Some of the recipes in this book come from European Countries, where metric measurements are used. I myself always work in pounds and ounces. North American readers will be more familiar with cups, where practical, I have put in the different measurements. However in some recipes, it spoilt the original flow of the writing and involved altering the prose style. So here is a table of basic measurements as a rough guide:

WEIGHTS

Metric	Imperial	American
25 gr	1 oz	
50 gr	2 oz	
125 gr	4 oz	1 cup (flour)
225 gr	8 oz (½ pound)	1 cup (sugar or fat)
500 gr	16 oz (one pound)	

LIQUID MEASURES

125 ml	¼ pint	½ cup
250 ml	½ pint	1 cup
500 ml	1 pint	2 cups

Author's Preface

The inspiration to write this book has been with me for a long time. I've always loved celebrating the Christian feasts of the different seasons as they come along, was fortunate enough to grow up in a family where such traditions were honoured, and have thoroughly enjoyed all the cooking and creativity of it in my own home since marriage.

But what perhaps prompted me to get on and *do* something about the book was the brochure that was sent to a headmaster friend from his local education authority. It announced the holding of a "Winter Festival Card Competition". Winter Festival? It turned out to be the new-style name for what we celebrate in December! These days, it seems, children are not supposed to call it Christmas but must give it a new name and only mark it in a strictly non-religious way.

That incident triggered off a warning bell in my mind. Unless we, as Christian families, work to foster a love of our Christian traditions and Christian culture in our country, something precious will have been lost forever.

Families trying to live as members of Christ's Church may well feel isolated and abandoned in today's Britain. So much militates against our way of living: easy divorce, the rock/pop culture, abortion-on-demand, the automatic use of swear-words on television, pornography leering at us from the shelves of newsagents, a self-indulgent attitude to life which too often ignores the plight of the poor. We need to bolster ourselves up by a renewed discovery of all the rich traditions of the Christian year, of celebrating together as families and communities the feasts and events that mark the most precious heritage of all: the Christian faith which has been the foundation of our civilisation.

I've written this book for Christian families who are not content to live in ghettoes but who see themselves as part of a wider community and as the inheritors of a rich glorious tradition. It's a book for sharing, as are the meals and celebrations it describes. Christian homes should be places of hospitality: the essence of our religion lies in sharing it with others.

My warmest thanks go to Father Michael Napier, of the Oratory, and to Iain Colquohoun, without whose generous help the

Author's Preface

publication of the first edition of this book would not have been possible. I also thank my husband Jamie for his encouragement, advice, and support.

Joanna Bogle

Christianity begins in Britain

How to use this Book

THE CHURCH has always known that the Christian message is best taught by "inculturation"—that is, by adopting and renewing local customs and traditions. The Christian message was first brought to Britain many many centuries ago. Its message of personal salvation, love, and justice challenged the ancient and terrifying pagan ideas of deity. It renewed people's lives and lifestyles. What had been the festival of the winter solstice became Christmas. The season of new growth in Spring became Easter.

As the centuries passed and new people invaded the islands and came to settle here it was necessary to Christianise Britain anew—the Angles and Saxons had driven the ancient Britons away to the remoter parts of the island—and so the faith was revived and the Christian traditions with it.

In modern times we face a new paganism. People worship crazy gods—money, sex, power, television, status. We need to make Christianity seem real, vital, and thrilling—and natural. The old traditions linger on, and the words "Christmas", "Easter", "Hallowe en", "Mothering Sunday", do still mean something. We must use these points of contact to inculturate the faith anew.

So this book isn't a prayer manual or a hand-book for family devotion. It's a series of suggestions for marking the seasons of the Church's year. There are prayers, songs, games, and special meals. There are ideas for things to make, and recite, and read about.

You're *not* meant to go through this book and say "Oh, so the Church says we must play charades at Christmas—I didn't know that", or "Gosh, I didn't know that parkin at Hallowe'en was compulsory" or "Fancy—we'll all have to play song-and-dance games on St John the Baptist's birthday!" You're meant to use the book with intelligence and a bit or perception, recognising the Christian beliefs which underlie it all but understanding that it's simply a guide to some of the customs and ideas that have grown up around them.

I need to make one or two explanations. First, to those Christians of non-Catholic denominations who will read the book: I hope you enjoy it and find it useful and won't be put off by the assumptions it makes about families' beliefs and practices. Secondly, to Catholics who may find that some of their own personal favourite devotions have been left out: "Oooh, there's nothing about Saint So-and-So". "Why, she hasn't even mentioned the Feast of Such-and-Such!" I've tried to stick to the fundamental framework of the Church's year— of course there is much more that could be added.

Finally, to Scottish, Welsh, and Irish readers who might justifiably be annoyed that this book is written from such an English angle. As soon as you start down the road of "inculturation", you come across local customs, local saints, local songs, local ideas, that bring the faith alive. I'm English and I've written this book primarily for people living in my own country. That means that people living in the other parts of the British Isles will find that a lot of it applies to them but some niggling bits don't. All I can suggest is that you thank God for a Church which can appeal to local diversity, and skip the pages about Saint George or about England being the Dowry of Mary as appropriate! I have, in any case, sought to introduce ideas from all over the world into the book at various stages.

One thing which might need a bit of explanation—there are occasional references to the "calendar change of 1752". This refers to the major alteration which was made in the organisation of our annual calendar in that year. Parliament decided to rationalise the calendar system and in doing so thirteen days were "lost". This produced a great deal of controversy at the time—there were even riots because people wanted to know what was to happen to those thirteen days! It meant that from henceforth certain feasts would be celebrated at different times. For instance, Christmas was still celebrated on December 25th, but now it was two weeks earlier. People gathered at Glastonbury in Somerset to see if the famous Glastonbury Thorn would blossom on the "new" Christmas Day and that year it didn't, so they felt they were vindicated in their conviction that the government was all wrong! And May— Hawthorn blossom—no longer blossomed in May after the Calendar change. Usually it is now June before the first tight green buds unfold and we know that summer is on the way, though we still call the blossoms "May".

The book begins with Advent, because that's the beginning of the Church's year. You will find each feast and season following in its logical place.

Of course, you can be a Christian anywhere. In Africa today, Christians are doubtless carving out new traditions and ceremonies linked with their own folklore. But this book was written for people living in England, who want to make the Christian faith come alive within the context of their own culture and with a sense of being linked with all the generations of Christian folk living in the same land who have gone before. It is meant to restore a sense of joy and pride in our own Christian culture, and of course anyone from any nation can share in any part of it.

Advent

O come, O come Emmanuel
And ransom captive Israel
That mourns in lonely exile here
Until the Son of God appear
Chorus: Rejoice, rejoice!
  Emmanuel
  Shall come to thee, O Israel!

O come, thou dayspring, come and cheer
Our spirits by thine advent here
Disperse the gloomy clouds of night
And death's dark shadows put to flight.

O come thou rod of Jesse, free
Thine own from Satan's tyranny
From death's dread hold thy people save
And grant them victory o'er the grave.

O come, O come, thou Lord of Light
Who to thy tribes on Sinai's height
In ancient times didst give law
In cloud and majesty and awe.

These days, the commercial rush of Christmas begins in September when shops start to sell Christmas cards and tinsel. By the end of October, many are fully decorated with frosting, plastic holly, Olde Worlde lettering, and inflatable Father Christmases.

One can either moan about this, and gripe about the nastiness of folk who are ruining Christmas with their money-making, or one can make a determined effort to renew and restore the real values of this holiest of feasts, starting with a proper Advent season.

Advent marks the four weeks before Christmas.

It is traditionally a season of penance and preparation before Christmas. The official Church liturgical colour is purple, symbol of penitence. Weddings used to be forbidden during this season—as also during Lent. But folklore and tradition have given their own flavour to each of the the Advent Sundays. The first is "Stir Up Sunday", so named because it is the day for "stirring up" the

1

How to make an Advent Wreath

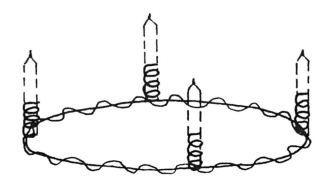

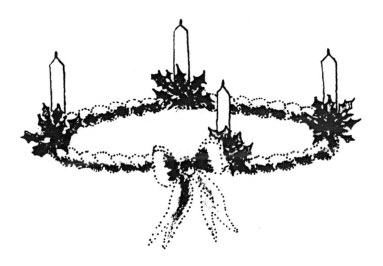

Christmas pudding. The third Sunday is "Gaudete Sunday", from the Latin word for "rejoice". On that day, everyone took a break from the penitential theme and pink vestments and altar-cloths were allowed in church.

It is a pity to start making preparations for Christmas before Advent has properly begun. The Autumn season has so many feasts of its own. When Advent finally arrives at the end of November, there are just four weeks to go until Christmas, and this is just long enough to make good preparations for the great feast and to enjoy doing so.

In Christian families, Advent should be taken seriously and used creatively.

"Stir Up" Sunday

The First Sunday of Advent is "Stir-up Sunday". The old Collect prayer for that day used to say: "Stir up—we beseech Thee, O Lord ..." and so by tradition it's the day when we "stir up" our Christmas cakes and puddings.

Everyone should take a turn at stirring the Christmas pudding. As you stir, make a secret wish. Don't breathe a word about it to anyone! It just may come true, but only if you preserve the secrecy.

There are all sorts of traditions about the tokens that go into the Christmas pudding. Many families put in money—washed and then wrapped in silver foil: shillings, pennies, and ha'pennies. Oh, alas, for the departed days of lovely sixpences and threepenny pieces! It's at times like Christmas that decimal coinage and expressions like "Five pea" sound so particularly nasty!

Others use silver charms, which you can buy specially: a button—whoever gets that is going to remain a bachelor at least for the forthcoming year, a shoe (a wedding on the way), a horseshoe (good luck), and so on.

Christmas Pudding

> ¼ lb flour
> 1 oz. chopped mixed peel
> 1 teaspoon mixed spice
> 1 teaspoon ground cinnamon
> half a teaspoonful ground ginger
> ¼ lb breadcrumbs

⅛lb shredded suet
¼lb brown or demerara sugar
one pound mixed dried fruit (raisins, sultanas, currants. Make sure the raisins are the seedless kind).
four eggs
juice and grated rind of one orange
juice and grated rind of one lemon
¼pint beer
¼lb black treacle
a dash of brandy
some milk
two peeled apples
a pinch of grated nutmeg.

Sieve all the dry ingredients in the bowl and mix together very thoroughly with the suet, breadcrumbs and sugar. Then, beat the eggs and add them, then add the treacle and the orange and lemon rind and juice and the beer and brandy. Chop the apples from the core and add them. Add the various fruits, and stir and stir and stir ... If the mixture seems too dry, pour in milk until it is comfortable to stir.

This size of pudding will need a 3-pint pudding-basin. You may prefer to make one 2-pint pudding and one much smaller 1-pint one which will be eaten later (at Easter for instance). You should buy cloth pudding-basin tops, put the mixture into pudding bowls, add a layer of grease-proof paper (the paper that butter comes wrapped in is ideal), fit the tops on, and boil for about four hours. If you cannot obtain cloth tops, silver foil will do, with string tied firmly under the bowl's ledge. When the pudding has cooled, store it somewhere until Christmas. On Christmas Day, boil it for a further two hours before serving.

Another Idea

An Australian relation—whose recipe for Ginger Log appears elsewhere in this book—sent me this attractive alternative to the traditional Christmas pudding. It could be made today and kept frozen. She wrote from Melbourne:

"Here is the recipe I use each Christmas instead of the traditional plum pudding as Christmas Day is often 140 degrees. It is called *Frozen Christmas Pudding.* You need 1 pint cream, 6 ozs icing sugar, 2 ozs cherries, 2 ozs crystalised cherries, 2 ozs mixed peel, ¼ cup chopped raisins, ¼ cup chopped sultanas, 4 egg whites, 1 dessert-spoon rum or brandly, 1 dessertspoon spice, 1 teaspoon cinnamon, 1 teaspoon nutmeg, 1 dessertspoon hot water, 1 dessertspoon cocoa.

"Soak fruit overnight with brandy. Beat egg whites stiffly with half the icing sugar. Beat cream with remaining sugar. Dissolve cocoa in hot water. Combine everything. Line mould with tinfoil, pour in mixture and freeze for as long as you like. This is enough for 6–8 people and it is VERY rich".

Mincemeat

You can also make your mincemeat today, and your Christmas cake. Mincemeat is nowadays just a delicious sweet mixture of different sorts of fruit and spices, but long ago it used actually to contain meat. It was a way of making meat specially tasty for Christmas— meat that perhaps was dry and tough because it had been salted to preserve it through the winter.

Mincemeat is very, very easy to make and requires no cooking. Have plenty of old jam jars washed and ready, with proper tops and labels (children will enjoy writing the labels, bearing the words "Mincemeat", and the date "Advent Sunday, 19??").

You put the following through the mincer, all mixed up together. Someone must keep turning the handle of the mincing machine while others steadily put things in at the top. You'll need a large mixing-bowl under the mincer where the mixture comes out!

> *a pound each of currants, sultanas, and seedless raisins*
> *half a pound each of dates (with stones removed) and mixed peel*
> *a carton of glace cherries*
> *a pound of peeled and chopped cooking apples*
> *¾ lb of shredded suet.*

When all these have been minced, add to the mixture:

> *a teaspoonful each of ground nutmeg and mixed spice and cinnamon,*
> *the juice and grated rind of one lemon and of half an orange*
> *a quarter pint of brandy.*

The mixture will then need a lot of stirring, at which, again, everyone can take a turn although I don't think mincemeat grants wishes like puddings do. You can add chopped peeled almonds to your mincemeat too if you like.

4

Crystallised Fruit Peel

My mother-in-law's delicious recipe creates a lovely form of sugary nibbles to enjoy over the Christmas season:

First save the skins of grapefruit halves from breakfast—keep them in the fridge or they get mildewed. Then:

Cut them into strips and remove the pith with a sharp knife.

Cover them with cold water and leave them overnight (this removes the bitterness).

Drain them, put them in fresh water and bring them to the boil. Then throw that water away. Repeat 3–6 times until the fruit is soft and semitranslucent (but still slightly crunchy).

Then pour off the final lot of water and weigh the fruit.

Put it back in the saucepan with an equal weight of granulated sugar. Cover it with water, stir it till the sugar dissolves and then boil it away gently until almost all the liquid is gone.

Have a flat open dish (a flan dish is ideal) full of sugar. Using tongs—the fruit is terribly sticky—roll the fruit strips in the sugar and set them aside to dry on a plate. The airing cupboard is a good place to dry them.

The sugared fruit will keep for about four months and is nicest if freshly used, so making it ready on Advent Sunday is about right. You can also use orange and lemon in addition to grapefruit.

Christmas Cake

Christmas cake is getting less popular these days, because our stomachs don't seem to have the capacity that our forefathers' stomachs had, and after a massive Christmas lunch few people can manage a slice of rich fruit cake at tea. However, most families agree that Christmas isn't Christmas without it.

> *10 ozs butter or margarine*
> *10 ozs soft brown or demerara sugar*
> *three tablespoonfuls black treacle*
> *grated rind and juice of one lemon and one orange*
> *five eggs two tablespoons brandy*
> *12 oz self-raising flour*
> *half a teaspoonful each of cinnamon, grated nutmeg, and mixed spice*
> *12 oz each of sultanas, raisins, chopped dates and currants*
> *4 oz chopped almonds*
> *5 oz glace cherries.*

You will need a nine-inch cake tin. Line the bottom and sides with foil or with greaseproof paper and grease it very thoroughly indeed with melted butter.

Beat the butter, sugar, treacle and the lemon and orange juice and peel together until soft and creamy. Beat the eggs with the brandy and add them. Sieve the flour and the various spices together and add these. Mix the fruit together and add. Stir very thoroughly. Put into the prepared tin and bake in a moderate oven for about 1½ hours. Then take the cake out, cover the top with greaseproof paper, and put it back in the oven on a lower heat for a further hour. Test it with a knife: if the knife comes out more or less clean, the cake is ready.

When it is cool, wrap it in foil until it is ready to be iced. If it seems dry, you can trickle sherry into it (For how to do this, see the section on Simnel Cake, for Mothering Sunday).

You ice it of course with thick white Royal icing over a layer of marzipan—and decorate it however you like.

The Advent Wreath

On the day before the First Sunday of Advent, it is time to make the Advent Wreath. There are lots of different ways of making one. Here is one way:
You will need:

> *About six feet of thick strong wire*
> *About ten feet of thinner green wire (the sort of wire covered in green plastic sold at gardening shops)*
> *pieces of evergreen branch—holly, pine, yew—whatever you like. You want branches about a feet long. Holly is painful to use but looks pretty.*
> *three purple candles*
> *one pink candle*
> *four red candles*
> *eight feet of purple or white ribbon*
> *eight foot of red ribbon*
> *wire cutters and scissors.*

Form the thick wire into a circle to form the basis of the wreath—you need it to be about one foot six inches to two feet in diameter, and two or three thicknesses of wire. Twist the ends together firmly.

From the green wire make four candle-holders by coiling the wire tightly round the bottom three inches of a candle and then fastening it to the main wire wreath structure. These candle-holders must be very tight, virtually cutting into the wax in order to hold the candles upright. It is no use just coiling the green wire once round the bottom of the candle and then fastening the ends to the thick wire: it must go round several times, to a height of about three inches up the candle.

You may actually find it easier to remove the candles while you fix on the greenery. You do this by bending the greenery round the wire base and fixing it there with the green wire. It is useful to have bits of the green wire cut in 6 to 8 inch lengths for this.

Cut two feet from the purple ribbon. Use the remaining four feet to coil round and round the wreath, pinning it in place at the front and cutting the ends into an inverted V shape and letting them hang down. Use the two ft. length to create an elaborate bow and pin this on top of the join, its ends similarly hanging down and with inverted Vs cut in them. Finally, slot into place the three purple candles and the one pink one. The purple candles and ribbon are for Advent—with one pink candle for Gaudete Sunday. On Christmas Eve you will remove the candle stumps and the wax-splattered ribbon (you can seize this opportunity to renew the greenery too, if you like), and replace them with red.

It is traditional to have the wreath hanging up, by ribbons, from the ceiling in the hall or main room. This certainly looks superb if it can be managed, but it is difficult to achieve—the thing tilts and won't balance, threatens to fall, drips wax everywhere, sways fearsomely in every breeze. We generally have ours on a small table by the window, the focal point of the room.

(See drawing at beginning of Chapter showing how to make an Advent Wreath)

How to use the Advent Wreath

You light one candle for the first Sunday of Advent, two for the next and so on. Gaudete is the Third Sunday in Advent. On that day—as with Laetare Sunday in Lent—the Church urges us to take a break from the solemnity of the season, and rejoice because of what is coming. The purple trimmings in church give way to rose-coloured ones. On Gaudete, we could have a foretaste of Christmas fare—perhaps the first sugary mince-pies.

The lights on the wreath are symbolic: Christ is our Light. We see Him coming, growing brighter and brighter as the weeks pass. We shall see this theme of Light again and again in the year—at Candlemas when we hear Him described as "A Light to Lighten the Gentiles", and at Easter when we light candles at the Easter Vigil and shout "Christ Our Light!"

"Advent" means "coming". We are waiting for Christ's coming—waiting with prayers and hopes, with excitement and longing.

Family prayers during Advent could be round the Advent wreath sometimes in the evenings. You may need to renew your candles if you want to light them every night, so well before Advent comes, stock up on purple and pink candles!

It is nice to do something special on the Sunday evenings of Advent. The glowing candles of the Advent wreath make a welcome for visitors. It is fun to invite some friends around to enjoy the little ceremony of the lighting of the appropriate numbers of candles, followed by the singing of carols, and the enjoyment of nuts, oranges, traditional spicey biscuits, and other snacks.

December Saints

One way of making Advent extra special is to celebrate each of the feast days that comes along in this period leading up to Christmas. Each has a message that helps us to appreciate Christmas more.

St Barbara—December 4th

St Barbara was an early Christian martyr. She died in the year 306. We do not know a great deal about her, but tradition says she was a young girl living in Nicomedia in Asia Minor, who became interested in Christianity. Her father strongly disapproved of this because he wanted her to marry a pagan prince. He locked her up in a tower and when she continued to hold fast to her new-found faith he dragged her out and had her executed. As he did so, a dramatic thunderstorm broke out and a great streak of lightning zig-zagged through the air, knocking him to the ground. For this reason, St Barbara is the patron saint of anything connected with thunderstorms, fire, gunpowder, electricity, or sudden loud noises! She is the patron saint, for instance, of the Royal Artillery! In some parts of Europe, miners have adopted her as their special patron, and burn special lights in her honour on her feast-day. It is also a day for letting off fireworks.

St Nicholas—December 6th

We mark the feast of St Nicholas on December 6th. He is, of course, well known as Santa Claus, and because his feast is in December, the celebrations have become all mixed up with Christmas. But in many parts of Europe—notably Germany, Holland and Austria—Saint Nicholas does not visit children's homes on Christmas Eve and put toys and gifts in their stockings. He comes on his own feast-day, December 6th—and he is not dressed in a red coat and fur-trimmed hood and warm boots but in his robes as a bishop. The tradition is that he visits homes on his feast-day, to see if the children have been good (sometimes he is carrying a large book in which all their good and bad deeds are written down). If they have been good during the past year, they get toys and sweets. If not, they get a cane! In some families, someone dresses up as St Nicholas, complete with mitre and crozier. In others, the children leave out their shoes by the fireside and find them filled later. St Nicholas is usually accompanied by a figure known as "Black Peter", a mischievous imp whose job it is to carry a bundle of canes for use on the naughty children. Sometimes St Nicholas is carrying a big sack, into which he will carry away the naughtiest children to dip them, it is said, in a giant inkpot!

In Britain, the idea of Santa Claus, or Father Christmas, is well established: he travels across the sky in a sleigh drawn by reindeer, and gets into houses either by having a door or window left open for him (and sometimes biscuits and milk left for him on the kitchen table), or down the chimney. Few things are more exciting for a child than the lumpy feeling of a stocking all filled with exciting things on Christmas morning! But who was the original St Nicholas? Did he really exist, or is it just a legend?

He most certainly existed and was a bishop in the fourth century, at a place called Myra in Asia Minor. He is supposed to have been one of the bishops present at the first general council of Nicaea. He is the patron saint of children—because he was always very kind to them—and also of sailors, and of pawnbrokers! Legend says that he helped three girls to get married by providing dowries for them— three bags of gold. You do not see many pawnbrokers' shops in modern Britain, but any that do still exist will probably have a sign showing three gold balls hanging in front of them.

The relics of St Nicholas are at Bari in Italy—they were taken there from Myra in 1087.

The devotion to St Nicholas which spread so widely and has become so much a part of European wintertime traditions shows the strength of Christian culture. It is sad that today, all our Christian Christmas-time traditions are being forgotten in the mad rush to spend money on expensive presents. How many modern British children know about the original St Nicholas and how he came to be associated with giving presents to children?

Celebrating St Nicholas

It might be fun to celebrate the Feast of St Nicholas by telling the story of his life at supper, and then having the children leave out their shoes by the fireplace overnight, to see if they are filled with sweets and biscuits—or with a cane!—in the morning. The biscuits should include traditional pfeffernüsse.

I don't see that this precludes St Nicholas from visiting again on Christmas Eve and filling stockings. Incidentally, the proper tradition for Santa Claus on Christmas Eve is that he fills *stockings* with *small toys and nicknacks*—not pillow cases with expensive gifts. It's surely better for children to know and understand that "big" presents come from fathers and mothers and aunts and uncles and grandparents, because these people love them and are loved in return? They can then enjoy the essence of present-giving and what it represents. Lots of gifts just materialising at the end of a bed is not the same: they should be *given*, and be seen to be given.

Traditional things to put in stockings on Christmas Eve include:

an orange or tangerine, chocolate coins in a little bag (remembering the bags of money that good St Nicholas gave for the three impoverished girls who were desperate to be married but had no clothes or food and couldn't meet anyone nice), a new penny, (or an old one polished up), a sugar mouse, a chocolate watch, a carnival "hooter" that unfurls as it blows and has a feather on the end, an apple, some nuts, *small* toys (card games such as "Donkey" and "Snap" and "Happy Families", a little fairy doll for a girl, wind-up clockwork toys, model soldiers).

An Irish nun told me that in Ireland it is traditional also to have a piece of peat in your stocking—representing fuel and prosperity for the coming year. A German gift is an apple with a coin stuck in it, or a marzipan pig with a (chocolate) coin in its mouth.

On both December 6 and Christmas Eve Santa Claus could be left a glass of milk (or whisky, on Christmas Eve), a carrot for his reindeer and something to nibble on (on Christmas Eve, a mince pie).

People who agonise over "when children should be told that Santa Claus isn't real" worry, I think, too much. Most of us as children had a suspicion about him—how did he manage to get round the *whole world* in just 24 hours, using only reindeer? So long as nobody goes on and on trying to convince children that he is a literal physical person who comes barging into their homes at night, most children recognise the general idea sooner or later and join in the spirit of the thing without worrying too much.

The "Boy Bishop" Tradition

Long ago in England, boys at choir-schools associated with cathedrals and monasteries elected one of themselves as a "boy bishop" on St Nicholas Day. The boy was fitted out with a complete set of bishops' vestments, and solemnly presented with a mitre and crozier, and he held office until Holy Innocents Day (December 28th). The idea was partly to teach the children about the office and duties of a bishop, and the boy concerned was expected to learn all about the great ceremonies of the Church, by acting out a bishop's part in them. But he could also ensure that everyone had plenty of fun during his period of office: he could announce holidays and treats, and call for distributions of sweets and gifts. To be elected "boy bishop" was a great honour, and it usually went to the boy who was felt to be most deserving: he also knew he had to work hard as he was expected to preach a proper sermon—in the presence of not only his fellow-pupils but also his schoolmasters and all those in the cathedral community—and to make all the proper responses at the various ceremonies in Latin. Some cathedrals in Britain still have a set of "boy bishop's robes" dating from these Medieval times.

A full St Nicholas Ceremony

If you want to have a full St Nicholas ceremony on December 6th, and can persuade some one to dress up as the saint in full episcopal robes (a mitre could be made out of cardboard, and a curtain would do as a cloak, with perhaps a walking-stick as a crozier) here is a description of how it used to be done in South-Western Austria:
"The children welcome the saint with a hymn; then he goes to a table and makes each child repeat a prayer and show his lesson-books. Meanwhile Rupprecht [he seems to be the same character as 'Black Peter'] in a hide, with glowing eyes and a long red tongue stands at the door to overawe the young people. Each child kneels before the saint and kisses his ring, whereupon Nicholas bids him put his shoes out of doors and look in them when the clock strikes ten. After this the saint lays on the table a rod dipped in lime, solemnly blesses the children, sprinkling them with holy water, and noiselessly departs. The children steal out into the garden, clear a space in the snow, and set out their shoes; when the last stroke of ten has sounded they find them filled with nuts and apples and all kinds of sweet things."
(Clement A. Miles, *Christmas Customs and Traditions*).

12

Food for December 6th

Spicey biscuits are the proper thing to eat on St Nicholas' Day, and they will also be nice to have for those candle-lit evenings around the Advent wreath. Apples, nuts, and marzipan are also traditional St Nicholas' fare. German *lebkuchen*—little honey-cakes, frequently made in the shapes of hearts and covered with sugar or chocolate—and *stollen* would be nice to have at tea-time. Stollen used to be a speciality of Dresden: it is a sweet yeast bread with dried fruits, mixed peel and almonds in it. In appearance it is like a long roll, thickly dredged with icing-sugar—it is said to represent the Christ-child, all wrapped up in his swaddling clothes.

Pfeffernusse (Ginger nuts)

14 oz. flour
3 level teaspoons baking powder
12 oz. granulated sugar
2 eggs
6 tablespoons milk
a pinch each of ginger, ground cloves, nutmeg, and white pepper
1 teaspoonful cinnamon
the grated peel of half a lemon and half an orange
1 oz. grated almonds
half an ounce of candied lemon diced very small
Icing: 4 oz sugar with 3-4 tablespoons hot water mixed until this is syrupy in consistency

Mix the flour and baking powder, and sieve onto a board. Make a hollow in the middle. Add the eggs, sugar, milk, and spices, and work in part of the flour. Distribute the rest of the ingredients throughout this mixture, and knead a smooth dough. Roll out 1 cm thick, and cut out discs between 2 and 3 cm in diameter. Put on a greased tray, and bake in a preheated oven. Ice when cold.

Heat: 175°C. Time: around 20 minutes.

Dresdner Christollen

14 oz raisins
4 oz currants
2 oz candied lemon peel

2 oz candied orange peel
8 oz ground almonds
2 liqueur glasses of rum
1 ½ llb plain (all-purpose) flour
3 ½ oz yeast
slightly less than ½ pt milk
8 oz butter. For brushing on afterwards: 3 oz butter. For sprinkling:
2 oz icing sugar

Crumble the yeast, and mix with the luke-warm milk. Add to the flour together with the soft butter and sugar, and knead into a smooth dough. Cover and leave to rise in a warm place for 20 minutes. Add the fruit that has been steeped in the rum. Knead thoroughly once again, and let the dough (covered) rise for another 30 minutes. Knead once more. Roll out on a surface covered with a little flour to make an oval slab about 3 cm. thick. Make a groove with a large rolling pin along the length of the centre of the dough, and then fold one half over the other. Let the Stollen rise for another 15 minutes on a greased baking tray. Bake for 20 minutes in an oven pre-heated to 200°—and then for 70 minutes at 175°. If the Stollen gets too brown, cover with some greaseproof paper. Immediately after baking, brush the Stollen with melted butter and sprinkle thickly with icing sugar.

Königsberger Marzipan (Königsberg marzipan)

250 gr. almonds
250 gr. icing sugar
1 egg-white
1 tbsp. rose water.

Dry the shelled almonds well, and put through the grinder twice. Mix with the egg-white and rose water to form a smooth paste. Leave to stand overnight. Form little pretzels, rolls, and loaves out of this bulk marzipan. Brush these with egg-yolk, and put on a baking tray covered with greaseproof paper. Roast fast with the oven set to a high temperature so that the marzipan quickly turns brown.

St Lucy—December 13

St Lucy's feast on December 13th is another festival of lights and candles that falls during Advent. It is celebrated particularly in Sweden, and is becoming better known in the rest of Europe too.

14

St Lucy was a young Sicilian girl, who died for her Christian beliefs in the 4th century, when the Roman Emperor Diocletian was slaughtering many people for their refusal to give up their faith. Her name means "light".

In Sweden St Lucy's day is simply known as "Lucia" and it is celebrated in almost every family, school, office, or community. A young girl, dressed in white and with a crown of candles on her head, distributes coffee and cake. I asked the Royal Swedish Embassy for more information on the custom, and received a detailed letter with information:

"At early dawn the 'Lucia bride' wearing a crown of lit candles and her bridesmaids, dressed in long, white gowns, go singing from household to household and serve steaming hot coffee and oldfashioned buns, called 'Lucia cats' or 'Lussekatter'.

A foreigner in Sweden might be surprised when he sees a blonde and fair girl in white with a candle crown on her head, and carrying a coffeepot and tray with cookies at four o'clock in the morning while walking through the city streets. But to Swedes, the sight is familiar in the longest night of the year.

Lucia has deep traditions in Sweden and has in fact been celebrated since the Middle Ages in many parts of the country, especially in the provinces of Västergötland and Värmland. Nowadays, it is the custom to hold Lucia festivals all over the country. Lucia contests are held in many communities and a beautiful girl is selected to wear the crown.

The Lucia legend, or rather legends, because there are so many versions of it, originated in Syracuse in Sicily around the year 300. According to one version, Lucia, which means bringer of light, was a beautiful young Christian girl, who was going to get married to a rich man. Before the wedding, she turned her whole dowry over to the poor in her village. Her betrothed becoming suspicious that she was a Christian, turned her over to the Roman prefect. She was imprisoned and tortured, her eyes gouged out with spears. She was condemned to death by burning, but the flames did not touch the martyr at the stake, and finally her prosecutors had to resort to the sword. The girl from Syracuse was declared a saint when Christianity had spread throughout the old Roman Empire and the 13th of December was dedicated to Lucia, who gave to the poor and then gave her life for her faith.

Another version related that Lucia had very beautiful eyes with which a heathen youth fell in love. Lucia tore them out and gave them to the young man, who thereupon became converted to Christianity. God then gave Lucia still more beautiful eyes than the ones she had given away.

Her name is undoubtedly closely related to the Latin word lux, meaning light. Research has not explained the significance of this similiarity in names, but in any case, Lucia is closely connected in Nordic folk tradition with live flames."

The Embassy also sent me a recipe for the saffron buns:

Saffransbröd (Saffron bread)

3–4 large plaits
or 2–3 rings
or about 30 rolls
2–3 packets saffron
1 oz, yeast (2 packages active dry yeast or 2 cakes compressed yeast)
1 pint
5–6 oz. butter or margarine
½ teaspoonful salt
5–8 oz. sugar
1 egg
scant 1¼ lb. plain flour
FLAVOURINGS:
2¼ oz. blanched, chopped almonds
3½ oz. raisins
2½ oz. chopped mixed peel
FOR BRUSHING AND DECORATING:
egg
crushed loaf sugar and chopped almonds or raisins

Plaits, rings: 200°C (390°F) 20–25 min.
Large saffron rolls: 225°C (435°F) about 10 min.
Small saffron rolls: 250°C (480°F) 5–6 min.
Dry the saffron stamens in a slow oven and pound them with a sugar cube. (Powdered saffron may be added directly to the tepid milk.) Crumble the yeast in a mixing bowl and cream it with a few tablespoonfuls of the milk.
Melt the fat. Pour the milk onto the fat and warm until tepid if necessary. Add the saffron.
Pour the milk onto the yeast and stir in the salt, sugar, about half the flour, the egg and the selected flavourings. Add the remaining flour gradually and work the dough until cohesive, smooth and

16

shiny. Sprinkle a little flour on top, cover with a cloth and allow the dough to rise until doubled in size.

Knead the dough in the bowl first of all. Then turn it onto a lightly floured baking table and knead it until smooth.

Divide the dough and shape it into plaits, rings, small buns or traditional shapes.

Put the shaped bread onto greased baking sheets and allow to rise. Brush with egg and sprinkle with sugar and almonds or decorate solely with raisins.

Bake.

Night falls, its darkness dread
Rich and poor steeping;
From earth the sun is fled,
Shadows are creeping
When to a darkened world
Comes with new light unfurled
Sancta Lucia, Sancta Lucia.

Hope glimmers through the gloom;
New life is stirring
In every silent room
Soft as wings whirring.
Lo, o'er the threshold—bright,
White-robed, with candle-light,
Sancta Lucia, Sancta Lucia.

"Shadows swift wing shall take
From earth's vale darkened"—
We to the words she spake
In wonder hearkened.
Now shall a glad new morn
Rise in a rosy dawn,
Sancta Lucia, Sancta Lucia.

Christmas

Come, come, come to the manger
Children, come to the children's king
Sing, sing, chorus of angels
Stars of morning o'er Bethlehem, sing.

The Crib

Christians have been making models of the manger, creating tableaux and acting out the Nativity scene since the very earliest days of the Church. But it is said that St Francis of Assisi first popularised the idea of the Christmas crib: that little model stable-scene with Mary and Joseph, shepherds, kings, ox and ass and star that has been re-created so many times since.

Making a model of the Bethlehem scene seems such an obvious and attractive thing to do at Christmas that it is not difficult to see why it has continued to be so highly popular.

You can make a splendid Christmas crib from an old wooden seedbox. Ask your local greengrocer for one, or any local keen gardeners that you know. We saw ours in a neighbour's dustbin and he was only to happy to let us fish it out and keep it!

Remove two corner-pieces diagonally opposite one another, and then, using a strong hacksaw, cut the box diagonally from corner to corner. You now have two potential model stables, so give one to a friend.

Stand the half-box up so that its former floor is now the back wall and its former sides the sloping roof. On the inside of the back wall, glue a square of dark blue paper on which you have glued some stars cut out from silver foil. This is the stable's rear window. Stick around it struts of wood to form a window-frame and cross-pieces. You make all these from the discarded corner-pieces of the seed-box, cut and trimmed. You can even make small curtains from scraps of cloth and glue them on, too, if you like.

Cover the sloping roof of the crib with greenery, and add tufts of cotton wool for snow, and some glitter or pieces of tinsel if liked. Fix a silver star onto a thin wooden strut (a lolly-stick would do) and fasten this to the back of the crib so that the star sticks up just over the point of the roof. This is how you make the star:

Cut two identical triangles—each side 1½ inches in length—out of stiff cardboard and cover them with silver foil (simply fold the foil over each triangle and staple it on—only one side of each triangle has to look right). Then put the two triangles on top of one another and you have a six-point star. Staple it firmly together.

A variety of inexpensive crib figures are on sale at Christmas: we actually bought ours through mail order from an advertisement in a Christian newspaper. We also bought, from an ordinary shop, some tiny plastic Christmas angels, which we strung on cotton threads and hung over and around the crib and from the points of the star. Incidentally, you could also string your star on to a thread and hang it over the crib from the ceiling if you don't want it sticking up on a wooden strut.

How to use the Crib

The crib could be erected on Gaudete Sunday in some suitable corner of the room. It is nice to have a candle on either side of it (making sure they are well away from the greenery). But not all the figures go into it yet. The manger remains empty—the Christ Child is not yet born. The figure should be kept in a drawer or cupboard and only put in its place at the centre of the scene after Midnight Mass or on Christmas morning. And the Three Wise Men should be placed some distance away from the stable scene, and can advance very slowly, by degrees, a little bit every day, so that on the feast of the Epiphany they finally get there.

Although the Crib is still empty of its most important occupant, the first evening that it is erected is one of beauty and enchantment—a herald of things to come, a whisper of Christmas. We can turn out the lights, light the candles on the Advent wreath and on either side of the crib and say prayers together or sing carols softly in the glow.

Carol Singing

There is nothing more Christmassy than sitting at home on a wintry evening and hearing voices carolling outside your front door, then opening the door to see a ring of cheery faces, exchanging greetings and passing on some money, and hearing them go off further up the street, the sound getting fainter.

Alas, carol singing isn't often as charming as that. You get two youngsters arriving in early November, shrieking hoarsely "We-wish-yer-a-merry-Christmas" with only the faintest of musical undertones, hammering on the door and being rude when you tell them they are at least a month too early.

Properly done, carol singing can be hugely enjoyable and give a great deal of pleasure. Plan ahead. Decide which charity will benefit from the money you raise and get some leaflets from them so that these can be handed out. Use the leaflets, too, to decorate jam-jars for collecting boxes. Prepare several of these—it is no use just having one if you are planning a big group of singers.

Borrow—with permission!—a large stack of hymn-books from a church, making sure that they have all the popular carols in them. Do check what hymn-books you use. One very irritating book that was used in our parish annually at one stage had "Still the night/Holy the night" instead of the more usual "Silent Night", and muddled up words of several other carols too.

It is very much better to have hymn-books than to try messing about with sheets of paper on a dark and windy night.

Collect together some torches (or even a lovely old-fashioned lantern if you can find one). Lash one of them firmly to the top of a tall pole.

Send out a photocopied letter to all friends who might like to join in— stressing that the evening will include a couple of hours of carol-singing around the neighbourhood followed by hot wine punch, soup, sausages and mince-pies at home. The letter should give full details of when and where to meet, with train information, etc. Choose somewhere that is easy to reach. Also invite neighbours and local friends. Don't bother to ask people who will not be prepared to come and *sing*. Tell everyone to dress warmly.

Prepare the food beforehand so that the soup and punch will only need reheating and the mince-pies popping into the oven. Just before you set out, put the sausages into the oven on a very low heat indeed so that they cook while you are singing.

Ask people to be prompt. As they arrive give them a drink. Before setting off, have a brief practice just to get people into the singing mood. The drink helps!

Map out a rough route through the local neighbourhood. Get the group to stand under a lamp-post and sing. While two or three collectors go to the houses within earshot. Give people a really good song for their money, then move on.

20

There are other carol-singing ideas. One group from a school went in Victorian costume: this was fun (they used the school's drama costumes), and with plenty on underneath they were also warm. If you make a picturesque group you could contact the local paper and get them to take your photograph and report how much you raised.

It's not a good idea, in my experience, to get fancy ideas about what you'll sing. People like the old favourites, and clever descants and partsongs that sounded lovely indoors lose a lot when hurled into a winter wind on a noisy corner.

If you have people who honestly can't sing, they can do the collecting. But only if they really are hopelessly flat or out-of-tune: basically, the rule must be that everyone who comes, comes to sing.

Carol singing should not happen before Gaudete Sunday, and the nearer to Christmas the better.

May I just add here that I think the meanest sort of carol-singers are those who come round with carols on a tape-recorder blaring out through a loudspeaker on a van driven slowly down the centre of the street? This effortless, charmless way of raising money seems to me empty and a sham. The whole point of the exercise is not just to raise cash, but to pass on Christmas joy and cheer with a personal message. We found, when we were carol singing, that it was well worth giving an extra song to an elderly person living alone and stopping for a proper chat: that is what the whole thing is really about.

A good day on which to go carol-singing would be December 21, which used to be St Thomas' Day until the Church revised the calendar in the 1960s. In past centuries in England, poor folk went "Thomassing", asking for alms for Christmas, on this day.

Christmas Decorations

> *Deck the halls with boughs of holly*
> *Fa-la-la-la-la, la la la la.*
> *'Tis the season to be jolly*
> *Fa-la-la-la-la, la la la la.*

Properly speaking, Christmas decorations—the Tree, the mistletoe under which everyone will kiss, the holly over the pictures and the crepe paper garlands—should not go up until Christmas Eve. Because shops now decorate themselves for Christmas pretty well as soon as the summer season is over, there is pressure for families to do the same. I have seen Christmas tree lights twinkling from suburban windows as early as October: how sick such a family must be of the sight of tinsel by December 25! People now sometimes even write to newspapers to point out the absurdities: "I saw my first Father Christmas on September 30th—is this a record?"

If Christmas Eve is just making for a little too much last-minute chaos, then December 21 is a good date. But on no account should decorations go up while we still have the major part of Advent to enjoy and share.

The Blessing of a Christmas Tree by Damasus Winzen, OSB

O God come to my assistance.

O Lord make haste to help me. Glory be to the Father and to the Son and to the Holy Spirit. As it was in the beginning, is now and ever shall be, world without end. Amen!
Then shall all the trees of the forest exult before the Lord, for He comes. Sing to the Lord, a new song; sing to the Lord, all you Lands.
Sing to the Lord; bless His name; announce his salvation day after day.
Tell His glory among the nations; among all peoples His wondrous deeds.
For great is the Lord and highly to be praised; awesome is He, beyond all gods.
Splendour and majesty go before Him; praise and grandeur are in His sanctuary.
Give to the Lord, you families of nations, give to the Lord glory and praise; give to the Lord the glory due His name.
Bring gifts, and enter His courts; worship the Lord in holy attire.
Tremble before Him, all the earth; say among the nations: the Lord is king.
Let the heavens be glad and the earth rejoice; let the sea and what fills it resound; Let the plains be joyful and all that is in them.
Then shall all the trees of the forest exult before the Lord, for He comes; for He comes to rule the earth.
He shall rule the world with justice and the peoples with His constancy.
Glory be to the Father and to the Son and to the Holy Spirit.
As it was in the beginning, is now and ever shall be, world without end. Amen.

22

Lesson from Isaias the Prophet: Thus saith the Lord: The land that was desolate and impassable shall be glad, and the wilderness shall rejoice and shall flourish like the lily. It shall bud forth and blossom and shall rejoice with joy and praise; the glory of Libanus is given to it: the beauty of Carmel, and Sharon, they shall see the glory of the Lord and the beauty of our God.

Thanks be to God.

And there shall come forth a rod out of the root of Jesse.

O Lord, hear my prayer.

And let my cry come to you.

Let us pray. O God who has made this most holy night to shine forth with brightness of the true light, deign to bless this tree—which we adorn with lights in honour of Him Who has come to enlighten us who sit in darkness and in the shadow of death. And grant that we upon whom shines the new light of Thy Word made flesh may show forth in our actions that which by faith shines in our minds. Through the same Christ our Lord. Amen.

(with thanks to the Wanderer Christmas Book, USA).

It will make it easier to wait for the decorations if Advent is spent doing interesting things: maybe making some Christmas presents and not just buying them, enjoying the candles on the wreath, planning some carol-singing, and doing some genuine spiritual preparation for the feast of Our Lord's birth. It seems right to go to Confession during Advent, and also to make some special spiritual efforts during this time: maybe a real commitment to family prayers together, using the crib as a focus. Or, in keeping with what is, officially, a penitential season in the Christian year, making some small sacrifices so that charity donations at Christmas are based on genuine self-giving.

St Boniface and the Christmas Tree

Today most of us associate Christmas trees with Germany. This is quite right, as that was where they originate. To this-day, German families' Christmas trees are decorated far more ornately—and with far more delicacy and seriousness—than those of their British counterparts the lighting of the candles on Christmas Eve is for them an event of great importance.

Long ago, pagans in the wild unconverted lands of Germany worshipped the trees and the forests. When the ramas missionary, St Boniface, came to bring them the Gospel, he taught them to worship the Creator, not the creation. It was he who first suggested to them the idea of decorating a tree in honour of Christ's birth at Christmas. Thorough this simple idea he was able to incorporate their old pagan idolatry into something far more noble and important.

Boniface was a Devon man—born at Crediton. He was christened Wynfrith, but took the name Boniface when he formally entered religious life as a young man. He took the Gospel to Bavaria, Westphalia, and Messe, becoming bishop of Mainz. He was martyred by pagan tribesmen at Fulda—where there is still a shrine to him. His feast-day is June 5th.

Christmas Eve

> *"Twas the night before Christmas, and all through the house*
> *Not a creature was stirring, not even a mouse ... "*

This is the most exciting and magical night of the year for children, and something of its special quality should spill over to adults, too.

On Christmas Eve, if you haven't done it before, write out that cheque to the charity you are going to support this year. The presents we exchange at Christmas are for love of Christ, and above all He wants us to help the poor and hungry and sick and lonely. There are plenty of people about at Christmas time reminding us that many people around the world won't be eating turkey and mince pies and having fun. You could hurry out and post the cheque before you settle down for the time of fun and feasting: if you never get around to sending it, Christmas won't be the same.

Mince Pies

You may have made mince pies already for carol singing, but on Christmas Eve you'll need to make plenty for the next few days. This is my mother's recipe. One Christmas my parents came to join us in Berlin, and my mother and I spent part of Christmas Eve making a big batch of pies to take along to the English church where the Army chaplain had arranged for various families to provide pies and glüwein for a celebration after Midnight Mass.

4 oz. butter
4 oz. flour
1 oz. sugar
1 egg
1 jar of mincemeat
sugar for sprinkling
small quantity of milk

Rub the fat into the flour, which you have mixed with the sugar. Use the egg to bind it all together, plus a small amount of milk as necessary, so that it forms a nice dough. Cut out with a crinkle-edged cutter, put into well-greased patty-pans. Put a teaspoonful of mincemeat in each and then cover with another crinkle-edged circle of pastry, sticking the edges firmly together with water. Sprinkle lightly with sugar and bake in a moderate oven until golden. If you use small cutters, this should make about two dozen pies.

Mince pies should always be round, never square or oblong. Traditionally, they are said to represent the manger at Bethlehem, with the Christ-child as the sweetness inside. Some people say that the dimpled edges are the hills and vales over which Mary and Joseph travelled on their way to Bethlehem and then on into Egypt.

This is a specially rich recipe, but of course you can make a cheaper version using lard instead of butter and omitting the egg and milk. Wholemeal flour is nicer than white flour in any recipe.

Celebrating Christmas Eve

In most of Europe, Christmas festivities begin on Christmas Eve. In countries where a Communist government has frowned on religion or even tried to crush it, Christmas and its message have survived through family culture. Polish families look for the first star in the sky as evening falls, and then begin their "Wigilia" or vigil meal. Straw is spread under the tablecloth to commemorate the Bethlehem stable, and then the best cloth is used on top. The feast includes dishes showing all the fruits of the earth: cabbage, beetroot, mushrooms, berries, bread topped with poppy seeds. No meat is eaten—a tradition dating back from the time not so very distant when Christmas Eve was by Church law and custom a day of abstinence. Fish is the central food, and some families try to have thirteen different kinds to represent Christ and the twelve Apostles. An extra place is always laid at the table for Our Lord, in the person of any passing stranger. The meal begins with the father of the family breaking the *oplatek*, the special Christmas wafer, and sharing it with his wife and so round the table with the whole family. Hugs and kisses are exchanged as each person shares in the wafer, emphasising peace in the home and mutual love. Pieces of *oplatek* may be posted to distant friends and relatives: Polish exiles in Britain post them back to families in Warsaw or Krakow.

In the Czech Republic and in Slovakia the traditional dish is carp. You buy it in the market and bring it home all wet and splashy and put it in the bath, and children go round to one another's homes: "Come and *see our* carp—it's simply huge!" Alex and Martha Tomsky, Czechoslovakians now living in Britain, described to me how they transform the main room of the house into the Christmas room, with presents stacked around the tree on the afternoon of Christmas Eve. Then, when everyone has just finished the special Christmas Eve supper in the kitchen, a grown-up sneaks out of the room and soon there is heard a mysterious ring on the door-bell. Who can it be? Could it be that the Christ-child has visited the house for Christmas Eve? Everyone troops into the living-room to what He has left . . .

In Germany, and Austria Christmas Eve is "der Heilige Abend", literally "Holy Evening", and the afternoon is spent getting everything ready. The main room is sealed off while it is decorated, the centrepoint being of course the tree with its straw stars, ring biscuits, foil and glass decorations, wooden angels, pine cones and chocolate and marzipan sweets. Sometimes a decorated plate of small goodies is prepared for each member of the family to nibble during the evening's celebrations: nuts, marzipan, lebkuchen, fruits, and biscuits. Some families tell children that it is the Christ Child Himself who decorates the Christmas tree: the tinsel being strands of the angels' hair which got caught in it as they helped Him. When everything is ready in the Christmas room, a small bell is rung and then everyone can go in. Sometimes carols are sung round the lighted tree before the present-giving, or the Christmas story read: sometimes children stand around the tree holding indoor sparklers and singing.

In Norway, Finland, and Denmark, the traditional Christmas Eve dish is a sweet creamy rice pudding, sprinkled with cinnamon and sugar and with melted butter poured over the top. In Sweden, families have a little ceremony known as "doppa i grytan", where everyone dips bread into the water in which the Christmas ham has been boiled, and then eats it. This dates back to the days when for poor families such a meal was a treat. For Swedish families, Christmas Eve is also the time for the visit of the *tomte* or Christmas gnome: he is a tiny fellow who is believed to live under the floorboards or out in the garden shed, the secret friend of all the family. He sneaks in to leave presents and then disappears. Presents are known as "julklappar" because one traditional way of leaving a gift is to toss it into the room and then hurry off, with a brisk knock on the door—the word "klappa" means to rap or knock.

Everywhere, there are special tales told about Christmas Eve: country people say that animals can speak with human voices at midnight, and another legend is that church bells can be heard ringing at the bottom of the sea.

Celebrating by candlelight, or by the lights from the Christmas tree, is part of the charm of Christmas Eve. In Britain, the traditional time for opening presents is Christmas morning: but it seems to me that many of the customs from other European countries are just waiting to be woven into our Christmas Eve.

An Old English Christmas

(from *"A Country Child"* by Alison Utley)

Joshua sat by the fire, warming his old wrinkled hands, and stooping forward to stir the mugs of mulled ale which warmed on the hob. The annual Christmas game was about to begin, but he was too old to join in it, and he watched with laughing eyes, and cracked a joke with anyone who would listen.

Margaret fetched a mask from the hall, a pink face with small slits for eyes through which no one could see. Then Becky put it on Dan's stout red face and took him to the end of the room, with his back to the others. Susan bobbed up and down with excitement and a tiny queer feeling that it wasn't Dan but somebody else, a stranger who had slipped in with the wind, or a ghost that had come out of the cobwebbed interior of the clock to join in the fun. She never quite liked it, but she would not have missed the excitement for anything.

Dan stood with his head nearly touching the low ceiling. His hair brushed against bunches of thyme and sage, and he scratched his

27

face against the kissing-bunch, to Joshua's immense satisfaction and glee.

Becky and Susan and Margaret stood with their backs to the fire, and Tom lay back on the settle to see fair play.

"Jack, Jack, your supper's ready." they called in chorus, chuckling and laughing to each other.

"Where's the spoon?" asked Dan, holding out his hands.

"Look all round the room," they cried gleefuly.

"Can't see it," exclaimed Dan as he twisted his neck round to the shuttered windows, up to the kissing-bunch and down to the floor.

"Look on top of All Saints' Church," they sang.

Dan turned his mask up to the ceiling.

"Lump of lead," he solemnly replied.

"Then catch them all by the hair of the head!" they shrieked, running and shouting with laughter.

Dan chased after them, tumbling over stools, catching the clock, hitting the row of coloured lanterns, pricking his neck, and walking into doors, cupboards, and dressers.

Susan ran, half afraid, but wholly happy, except when the pink mask came too near and the sightless eyes turned towards her, when she couldn't help giving a scream. Joshua warded him away from the flames, and Tom kept him from upsetting the brass and copper vessels which gleamed like fires under the ceiling.

Susan was caught by her hair and she became Jack. Now she put on the strange-smelling mask, and with it she became another person, bold, bad, fearless.

So it went on, the old country game, whilst Margaret kept stopping to peep in the oven at the mince pies and roast potatoes.

Next came "Turn the Trencher", but Dan couldn't stop to play for he had to be off a-guisering. He blacked his face with burnt cork and whitened his eyebrows. He borrowed Becky's black straw hat and wrapped her shawl round his shoulders. Then off he went to join a party of farm lads who were visiting the scattered farms.

He had not long gone, and Tom was spinning the trencher between finger and thumb in the middle of the floor, when the dog barked as if someone were coming.

"Whist, whist," cried old Joshua.

"Hark," cried Tom, stopping the whirling board, "there's something doing."

They heard muffled steps coming down the path to the door.

"It's the guisers coming here," cried Tom, and they all stood up expectantly with eager faces and excited whispers.

Here we come a-wassailing
Among the leaves so green,
Here we come a-wandering,
So fair to be seen.

We are not daily beggars
That beg from door to door,
But we are neighbours' children,
Whom you have seen before.

Call up the butler of this house,
Put on his golden ring,
Let him bring us up a glass of beer,
And better we shall sing.

Here they pushed open the door and half entered.

God bless the master of this house,
And bless the mistress, too,
And call the little children
That round the table go.
And all your kin and kinsfolk
That dwell both far and near,
I wish you a Merry Christmas,
And a happy New Year.

"Come in, come in," shouted Tom, with his broad face wreathed in smiles. Half a dozen young men and a woman stamped their feet and entered, bringing clots of snow and gusts of the sweet icy air. Their faces were masked and they disguised their voices, speaking in gruff tones or high falsettos, which caused much gay laughter.

They stood in a row in front of the dresser, and asked riddles of one another.

"How many sticks go to the building of a crow's nest?"

"None, for they are all carried."

"When is a man thinner than a lath?"

"When he's a-shaving."

"Who was the first whistler, and what tune did he whistle?"

"The wind, and he whistled 'Over the hills and far away'."

"What is that which a coach cannot move without, and yet it's no use to it?"

29

"A noise."

Tom and Joshua knew the answers and kept mum, but Becky and Susan were busy guessing, Margaret too.

Then Tom said, "Now I'll give you one.

> *"In a garden there strayed*
> *A beautiful maid, as fair as the flowers of the morn;*
> *The first hour of her life she was made a wife,*
> *And she died before she was born."*

The guisers made wild guesses and Tom sat back, smiling and gleeful.

"No, you're wrong, it's Eve," he said at last in a tone of triumph. "And here's another," he continued:

> *"There is a thing was three weeks old,*
> *When Adam was no more;*
> *This thing it was but four weeks old,*
> *When Adam was four score."*

The guisers gave it up, and Susan, who had heard it many a time, could scarcely keep the word within her mouth, but Tom frowned and nudged her to be quiet.

"'Tis the moon," he cried, and they all nodded their masks.

"Here's one," said Joshua:

> *"I've seen you where you never were,*
> *And where you ne'er will be;*
> *And yet with in that very place,*
> *You shall be seen by me."*

When they couldn't guess it and had murmured, "You've seen me where I never was" many times, he told them, "In a looking-glass".

"Eh, Mester Taberner," cried one. "You've never seed me in a looking-glass," and they all guffawed.

"And I know that voice," returned Joshua, "'tis Jim Hodges from Over Wood way."

"You're right, Mester Taberner," said Jim, as he removed his mask and disclosed his red cheeks.

So the guessing went on, until all the mummers were unmasked, Dick Jolly, Tom Snow, Bob Bird, Sam Roper, and Miriam Webster.

They drew up chairs to the fire and Susan got plates and big china mugs, and the two-handled posset cups. Margaret piled the mince pies, as big as saucers, on the fluted dish and handed them round.

"Help yourselves, help yourselves, 'Christmas comes but once a year, and when it comes it brings good cheer,'." said Tom, and he poured out the spiced hot ale for the men, and the women ate posset with nutmeg and sugar.

Mulled Ale

"Make some ale quite hot, and add a little grated nutmeg or mixed spice. For each quart of ale beat up half-a-dozen eggs and mix with a little cold ale, then pour the hot into it and empty from vessel to vessel several times to prevent curdling, for the space of a *Pater* and five *Aves*.

Stir over the fire till sufficiently thick, add a piece of butter or a dash of brandy, and serve with dry toast."

I got this from *A Christmas Book* by D.B. Wyndham Lewis and G.C. Heseltine, published in 1928. The recipe is initialled "R.M." and is undated. I have not tried it.

A Christmas Truce

In 1914, during the first Christmas of the First World War, German and British soldiers, sitting only yards away from each other in their trenches, began singing carols to one another. Then some of them clambered out of the trenches, walked across No Man's Land, and began to exchange greetings, and drinks, and handshakes. Family photographs were displayed, and letters. It was Christmas Eve. This happened along lengthy stretches of the Western front: it was the last glimpse of Old Europe before the slaughter that ushered in a new era.

A correspondent wrote in *The Times:* "We have all read what happened between the opposing armies, and how it came unexpected, undesigned, and yet willed with all the unconscious force of their natures. Not once or twice but again and again we hear of this sudden change upon the night of Christmas Eve, how there was singing upon one side answered by the other, and how the men rose and advanced to meet each other as if they had been released from a spell. Everyone who tells of it speaks also of his own wonder as if he had seen a miracle; and some say that the darkness became strange and beautiful with lights as well as music, as if the armies had been gathered together there not for war but for the Christmas feast."

(A. Clutton-Brock, writing in *The Times* quoted in *A Christmas Book*, 1928).

Christmas Day

Most people don't need to be reminded of what to do on Christmas morning. Children scrambling around in the early hours pulling things out of their stockings, a chaotic breakfast, the distribution of presents, church, the preparations for lunch—every family manages to work out its own routine.

Christmas Ideas

Some families find that Christmas gets a little stale when everyone is grown up: when what had been a household of excited children has turned into a household of adults and teenagers. It is at this stage that Christmas needs an extra effort, the introduction of new dimensions that stress the special nature of this feast and its real importance. This may be the time to welcome into our homes people who might have felt ill at ease in a house full of children but for whom we now have space and time: the elderly person living alone, the visitor from a distant country who cannot get back for Christmas. Try asking the local clergy if they know of anyone who might be having to spend Christmas alone.

The *Universe* newspaper in December 1983 printed a sad letter from a lady who would be spending Christmas alone—and the Editor was inundated with letters inviting her to share the holiday with families from every corner of the British Isles: a heart-warming display of people's natural generosity. But many lonely people are too shy or too proud to ask: you may need to go out and find them. Emphasise that they'll be doing *you* a favour: a guest at the Christmas table is what makes the feast into a real celebration, an excuse for the special decorations, Christmassy napkins, candles, crackers, toasts over the liqueurs.

Not that you need always wait until the children are older. Polish friends living in Surrey always invite a fellow Pole to their home for Christmas Eve, which they celebrate in the Polish style with all their country's old traditions. The father of the family met him by chance some years ago at the Polish club in London, and when the talk fell to Christmas, heard him say that, living alone and with no family in England (he was a refugee), he found Christmas Eve too full of memories and so always spent it at a cinema, seeing the programme round twice if necessary until it was time to go home. Then and there the invitation was extended to join in the family's celebrations: he

nt@,111 l

arrived to find a place waiting for him at the table and parcels bearing his name under the tree and has never spent a lonely Christmas since.

Why Turkey?

People often ask me why do we eat turkey at Christmas? And when did the tradition start? Mr George Chowdharay-Best, a researcher on many historical matters, has sent me useful information on this: "Turkey was widely established as a Christmas dish, often in association with beef, as early as 1573. In 1854 Londoners consumed over 100,000 of them, and a writer in *Leisure Hour* (15 December 1859) described huge numbers of turkeys in Leadenhall Market. Finally, J.L. Cowan in the *Overland Monthly* of San Francisco (november 1906) stated that 'in England the turkey raising industry is carried on to an extent never attempted on this side of the Atlantic'—odd, because in the U.S. turkey is I believe involved in Thanksgiving as well as at Christmas."

The turkey's native habitat seems originally to have been North America and Mexico. It is also associated with India however, the French call it a "coq d'Inde" or a "Dinde" and the Germans a "Kalikutische Hahn" or "Hen from Calicut"—Calicut being a place on the coast of the Indian sub-continent, South of Goa. Not to be outdone, people in Turkey itself call it a "Hindi"!

I suspect that its popularity at Christmas comes from the fact that the bird is tasty, & looks attractive with its white meat. People could also have been able to keep them in sheds near their houses, where they would have eaten up all sorts of fatty scraps. This is easier than keeping a cow alive on expensive winter fodder until December.

Christmas Games

After Christmas dinner (I think it is always called that, even if it's eaten at midday) it's traditional now in Britain for people to turn on the television or radio to hear the Queen's Christmas message. We always fill our glasses solemnly before the National Anthem begins, and then when the Queen has finished speaking, we stand and toast her health.

But it seems a great shame just to sit watching television all afternoon. Watching entertainment on TV is a poor substitute for doing things yourself, and contributes to that full, dissipated feeling which so often means that Christmas Day ends in anticlimax, bickering and bad temper—too much to eat and too little activity making a ghastly combination. Try these instead:

A Mime Game

I learnt this one at Coventry Cathedral. I was a teenager attending a summer youth conference there with people from different countries, and this game was played on our last night. No words were needed so once people got the hang of what we were meant to be doing the different languages didn't matter, and laughter is a common language.

Divide into two teams. One stays in the room and settles down comfortably with drinks and turkish delight and dates and chocolates to be the audience. The other, all but the leader, goes out of the room. The leader then has to think up which action he will mime. He tells the audience what it is: it can be something quite silly but it must be specific—an excellent one is washing an elephant. Other ideas might be decorating a bathroom, conducting a marriage ceremony (no supporting extras allowed), or chopping down trees and building a log cabin.

No props of any kind are allowed, and no words may be spoken. When the mime begins, the first member of the team is allowed in. He must watch the mime—not knowing what it is, of course—and then when it is over, repeat it while the next member watches, and so on. It's comic to watch the mime changing, and each team member becoming more and more baffled than the one before, repeating certain actions and gestures faithfully without understanding their meaning. Things get completely distorted as the mime goes on. At the end, everyone has to say what it was he thought he was doing: there will be a chorus of "Oh, I thought I was—" and so on. Then the team that has been audience has a go, convinced they will do a better job, which they won't.

This is really a game for goodish crowd—it starts getting ridiculously funny with about the fifth or sixth person repeating the mime.

The Scribbling Race

Again you're in two teams. But this time the organiser stands apart: he has prepared a list of things that must be conveyed by one member of each team to the others without use of words, either written or spoken. Each team has paper and pencil, and can draw as much as they like—they can also act in mime, but must not make any sound.

The leader of each team goes to the organiser and is told in a secret whisper the first thing that must be conveyed. Here is a sample list:

A blasted heath
The News
Peace
The bang inside a cracker
Incompetence
A gaggle of geese
Indigestion
The myrrh carried by one of the Magi
Danger

The team member who guesses correctly what the leader is trying to convey hurries to the organiser to be whispered the next item on the list. The winning team is the one which guesses the lot first.

Charades

The standard game which shouldn't need explaining. It's funniest if done silently. You show by gestures whether you are going to depict a book (hands depict open book) a play (draw a square in the air to indicate stage) a film (hand turns handle of camera) or a song (mime operatic singing). Then you hold up fingers to show the number of words that are to be conveyed, then show which word, and which syllable of it, you are now going to depict.

Example:
Northanger Abbey.
Book. Two words.

First word,
first syllable:
NORTH. *Act as if looking at compass. Point in a particular direction, and shiver, and point again, and walk off, shivering, in that direction.*

35

Second syllable:
ANGER. *Act angry. Pace up and down shaking fist and stamping.*

Second word.
ABBEY. *Indicate that you are a monk with a cowl over your head and a long habit. Fold arms as if tucked up in sleeves of habit. Adjust imaginary hood. Walk slowly with head bent. Genuflect and kneel in prayer.*

Other ideas for charades to set you off:
Books
A Tale of Two Cities
Mary Poppins (also a film)
Treasure Island
Little Women
Swallows and Amazons
The Lion, the Witch, and the Wardrobe
David Copperfield

Films	*Songs*
The Sound of Music	A Spoonful of Sugar
Doctor Zhivago	Rule Britannia
Gone with the Wind	London Bridge is Falling Down
Pollyanna	Little Bo Peep
Where Eagles Dare	My Old Man's a Dustman
Crocodile Dundee	Silent Night
	Come into the garden, Maud
	Cockles and Mussels

Consequences

Another old favourite that shouldn't need explaining. Dish out paper and pencils all round. At the top of the page everyone writes the name of a man, and then folds the page over and passes it to his neighbour. Next, everyone writes the name of a lady, folds it and passes it on. Then where they met. Then what he said. Then what she said. Then what happened next. Then what the world said about them. When they've been passed on for the last time you read them out one by one.

"Who Am I?"

Everyone chooses to be a character from history, without revealing who it is. Then a topic is announced, eg "Marriage" and each person must make an appropriate comment on it, in the style of the person they have chosen to be, and giving some clue as to his/her identity. For example, a person being Henry VIII could say, on the subject of marriage "Well, I've had plenty of experience of *that*", while some one who had chosen Jane Austen might say "I never married myself, but have recorded with some amusement the courtships and trials of others". When you have gone once round on the first topic, you choose others: Religion, Politics, Christmas, Children, Holidays, Hot Weather, Favourite Foods, Foreign Travel, Likes and Dislikes, Women's Fashions. The trick is to reveal something about your chosen character without giving too much away. You fall out of the game when your character is guessed. Every player is allowed three guesses to every other player. Winner is the last player left in. You can also play this game with characters from books.

Quiz

Finally, a Christmas Quiz for the family. This one's about old English customs and traditions, and all the answers will be found by reading this book. Alternatively, if you turn to the very back page of this book and hold it up towards the mirror, you will find the answers there.

1. In what year was the calendar changed in Britain so that we "lost" thirteen days?
2. "St Anne, she sits in the sun." Who is the St Anne mentioned, and why does she "sit in the sun"?
3. What is Twelfth Night?
4. What is the old name for the third Sunday in Advent, and what does it mean?
5. When is Hallowe'en?
6. What day is Candlemas?
7. When is Catterntide?
8. If someone asked you to "Remember the grotto" in July, to what would it refer?
9. What does the word "Carnival" actually mean? When is the traditional carnival time?

10. Why is New Year's Eve Called "Sylvester" in Germany?
11. From where does the name "Pentecost" come?
12. What was the old medieval title for England, which commemorated the devotion of English people to the Mother of God?
13. When is St John the Baptist's birthday?
14. In the song about the Twelve Days of Christmas, when did the true-love send some gold rings? When did he send some milkmaids?
15. Which saint is it on whose feast we all watch the weather to see if it will be rainy or sunny for the next forty days?
16. What is a Pace Egg?
17. Who was St Stephen?
18. Who was St Thomas a Becket?
19. We eat pancakes on Shrove Tuesday. But what does the word "Shrove" mean?
20. When is Collop Monday?
21. What is the traditional thing to do at Rogationtide? When is Rogationtide?
22. Why do we eat roast lamb at Easter?
23. What is "Maundy money"?
24. When is "Spy Wednesday"?

The Legend of the Glastonbury Thorn
A Story for Christmas

Who could fail to be thrilled by the legend of Glastonbury? It combines all the elements of mystery with the excitement of adventure. Its origins are lost—and there are many different versions of the tale.

Joseph of Arimathea

The New Testament tells us that Joseph of Arimathea, a wealthy member of the high Jewish council, the Sanhedrin, offered to take the body of Our Lord after the crucifixion and give it a decent burial in a tomb which he had prepared for his family use. So after the centurion standing at the foot of the cross had agreed that Christ was dead, the body was taken down and laid in this sepulchre, and a stone was rolled across the doorway. We know, of course, what happened next—the Resurrection and Our Lord's appearance to His disciples. But what did Joseph of Arimathea do? After his one gesture of friendship and help, he disappears from the scene, and the

38

New Testament does not mention him again. We assume that he simply went on living in Jerusalem.

But legend tells us that he became a Christian believer, and joined the other early Christians, including Mary Magdalene, and Lazarus, and suffered persecution from the Jews. They had to flee from the Holy Land because of this persecution, and eventually ended up in England, landing in a small boat on the West Coast. One version of the story says that Joseph of Arimathea was set with some others by the Jews in a small boat, without sails or oars, and left to drift in the sea: it is said they drifted to Marseilles in France, and went from there to England. Of course this is only a legend, but an attractive one.

The Twelve Hides

Joseph is said to have brought with him to England a precious relic: the very chalice which caught the blood and water which flowed from Our Lord's side at Calvary. This was the Holy Grail, and Joseph and his companions brought it to Glastonbury. He, with his eleven companions from France, built a small church of twisted woodwork filled in with clay. The king of this particular part of Britain in those days was Arvigus, and he gave each of the twelve a "hide" or area of ground, about 120 acres. There is still an area of land at Glastonbury called the "twelve hides".

Avalon

At the time of Joseph's arrival, Glastonbury was a wet and marshy area so that the church stood on what was virtually an island. The island was known as Avalon. The church was dedicated to Our Lady.

They had arrived at Glastonbury because the hill, Glastonbury Tor, was an obvious landmark in the region. And it is said that Joseph had been told in a dream to look for a hill "most like to Tabor's holy mount". The place where they first landed, weary and exhausted, is "Weary All" or "Wirral" and it was here that Joseph stuck his staff in the ground and it bloomed—the famous Glastonbury Thorn. This thorn-bush survived for centuries, eventually being uprooted by the Puritans in the 17th century. But a sprig was saved and the thorn now thrives anew in its current home in the grounds of Glastonbury Abbey. It blossoms every Christmas, and a sprig is cut and sent to the Queen.

King Arthur

Joseph of Arimathea buried the Holy Grail here at Glastonbury Tor, and also started to spread the message of Jesus Christ, converting many of the people living in the district and finding them unusually receptive to the message. These people of the ancient British race were living under Roman rule. Later, when the Romans left, chaos was to ensue—except that a British king, Arthur, Romano-British and Christian, kept a peaceful kingdom and through his Knights of the Round Table fostered ideals of Christian chivalry and order. His knights set off in quest of the Holy Grail, and found it buried here at Glastonbury. Much later King Arthur was wounded in battle somewhere around this district: his sword Excalibur was thrown into a lake where a hand rose up from the water to grasp it and take it to the depths, while Arthur was borne away on a barge into the mists of Avalon. At Glastonbury you can see the place which is supposed to be his grave. In the Middle Ages a body was found which was said to be his, together with that of his queen Guinivere (the name means True Queen) and they were buried in the nave of Glastonbury Abbey, up by the high altar. Tales of King Arthur abound in Britain and also across the sea in Brittany.

Is it all just legend? We do know for certain that there was an ancient wattle church at Glastonbury when the Saxons came, and that it had by then been a place of pilgrimage for many years. It was dedicated to Our Lady. We also know that for many centuries people have believed that Joseph of Arimathea is buried beneath the Tor. At the foot of the Tor you can visit the "Chalice Well" which is said to be associated with the Holy Grail.

It is said that St Patrick, who converted Ireland, may be buried at Glastonbury, too. He was, of course, a Romano-Briton like Arthur, and lived further along the western coast of Britain, the bit we now call Wales, which is not so very far away from Glastonbury. It is said that after his missionary years across the sea in Ireland, he was led by divine guidance to Glastonbury, where he ended his days.

St Dunstan

From the time of the arrival of the Saxons, legend gives way to fact. They were in due course converted to Christianity. They recognised that the small wattle church was of special, even unique, significance, and they seem to have gone to great lengths to preserve it, enclosing it within a stone church which was later to become the basis of a great monastery. St Dunstan was later to become Abbot here. The original wattle church burned down in a great fire which swept the abbey in 1184, to the great dismay of the monks who, written records tell us, had tended the old wattle building carefully as a place deserving a great veneration.

The monastery thrived during Saxon times. Three English kings were buried in its vaults: Edmund I in 946, Edgar in 975, and Edmund Ironside in 1016. The Norman invasion of 1066 brought changes, including the building of a new and bigger church, but this burned down in the disastrous fire of 1184 and a fresh start had to be made. On June 11, 1186 a splendid new building was consecrated covering the site of the old wattle chapel and extending to include a massive area. It included a church with a long nave and side-chapels, and later cloisters, rooms for the monks, a Chapter House where the whole community would meet together, kitchens, guest-rooms, and all the other trimmings of monastic life.

For centuries, this Abbey flourished as one of the great religious centres of England. It was the place for major celebrations and events, for pilgrimages and for festivities. But under Henry VIII it was destroyed along with all the other great religious houses of England. Its end was dramatic; the roof was hacked off, church furnishings and trimmings confiscated, buildings ransacked. The Abbot, Richard Whiting, was dragged through the streets of Glastonbury and executed publicly on the top of Glastonbury Tor.

The Tor had itself been a place of pilgrimage and is still today topped by the tower of a church dedicated to St Michael. From the top of the Tor you can gaze out across Avalon. Sometimes there is low-lying mist in the valleys. It is not hard to imagine what it all looked like when the area was a marshy set of islands, and the water shone like glass as it caught the sunlight (the name Glastonbury comes from "glass") and to recognise why so many legends and tales are bound up with it all.

41

The "Cradle"

Glastonbury has been called the "cradle of British Christianity". Certainly there was a Christian community here long before Augustine landed at Kent to convert the later arrivals, the Angles and Saxons. The ancient wattle church at Glastonbury was described by the Saxon King, Ima, as being the foremost Church in Britain, the fount and source of the nation's religion, the "old Church of the most Blessed Virgin". A writer in about the year 1000 says that when the Saxons arrived they found "a Church, not built by the art of man, but prepared by God Himself for the salvation of mankind, which Church the Heavenly Builder declared, by many miracles and many mysteries of healing, He had consecrated to Himself and to Holy Mary Mother of God".

The idea of a church "prepared by God Himself" lent itself to the notion that Christ Himself had visited Glastonbury. It is said that He came here on a trading trip—he was a carpenter, remember, and this was a major centre for obtaining tin—in those "hidden years" before His public ministry began when He was 30 years old. Legend says that He lived for a few months in a mud-and-wattle dwelling at Glastonbury while on a trip to the tin-mines of this Western coast of Britain. Was this little dwelling later rediscovered by Joseph of Arimathea and his companions and turned into a church?

It was the idea that Christ came to our island and spent some time on our shores that inspired the poet William Blake to write:

> *"And did those feet in ancient time*
> *Walk upon England's mountains green?*
> *And was the Holy Lamb of God*
> *On England's pleasant pastures seen?"*

Certainly Glastonbury retains its mystical significance for many. Christians come here on pilgrimage. There is a Shrine to Our Lady of Glastonbury in the town, not far from the Abbey Ruins. The ruins themselves, open to the public and well tended on their grassy lawns, tell the story of the great Abbey. The Tor, mysteriously dominating the landscape for miles around, looms over everything. People also come who are not Christians—Glastonbury has become a fashionable centre for folk of all sorts of beliefs including the occult. Why are such people so fascinated by it? Is it perhaps because it really is a holy place, a place specially important in the Christian story?

42

An American Pioneer Christmas

(from: *"Little House on the Prairie"*, by
Laura Ingalls Wilder)

The days were short and cold, the wind whistled sharply, but there
was no snow. Cold rains were falling. Day after day the rain fell,
pattering on the roof and pouring from the eaves.

Mary and Laura stayed close by the fire, sewing their nine-patch
quilt blocks, or cutting paper dolls from scraps of wrapping paper,
and hearing the wet sound of the rain. Every night was so cold that
they expected to see snow next morning, but in the morning they saw
only sad, wet grass.

They pressed their noses against the squares of glass in the
windows that Pa had made, and they were glad they could see out.
But they wished they could see snow.

Laura was anxious because Christmas was near, and Santa Claus
and his reindeer could not travel without snow. Mary was afraid
that, even if it snowed, Santa Claus could not find them, so far away
in Indian territory. When they asked Ma about this, she said she
didn't know.

"What day is it?" they asked her anxiously. "How many more
days till Christmas?" And they counted off the days on their fingers,
until there was only one more day left. Rain was still falling that
morning. There was not one crack in the grey sky. They felt almost
sure there would be no Christmas. Still, they kept hoping.

Just before noon the light changed. The clouds broke and drifted
apart, shining white in a clear blue sky. The sun shone, birds sang,
and thousands of drops of water sparkled on the grasses. But when
Ma opened the door to let in the fresh, cold air, they heard the creek
roaring.

They had not thought about the creek. Now they knew that they
would have no Christmas, because Santa Claus could not cross that
roaring creek.

Pa came in, bringing a big fat turkey. If it weighed less than twenty
pounds, he said, he'd eat it, feathers and all. He asked Laura,
"How's that for a Christmas dinner? Think you can manage one of
those drumsticks?"

She said, yes, she could. But she was sober. Then Mary asked him
if the creek was going down, and he said it was still rising.

Ma said it was too bad. She hated to think of Mr Edwards eating
his bachelor cooking all alone on Christmas day. Mr Edwards had

been asked to eat Christmas dinner with them, but Pa shook his head and said a man would risk his neck trying to cross that creek now.

"No", he said. "That current's too strong. We'll just have to make up our minds that Edwards won't be here tomorrow."

Of course that meant that Santa Claus could not come, either.

Laura and Mary tried not to mind too much. They watched Ma dress the wild turkey, and it was a very fat turkey. They were lucky little girls, to have a good house to live in, and a warm fire to sit by, and such a turkey for their Christmas dinner. Ma said so, and it was true. Ma said it was too bad that Santa Claus couldn't come this year, but they were such good girls that he hadn't forgotten them; he would surely come next year.

Still, they were not happy.

After supper that night they washed their hands and faces, buttoned their red-flannel nightgowns, tied their nightcap strings, and soberly said their prayers. They lay down in bed and pulled the covers up. It did not seem at all like Christmas time.

Pa and Ma sat silent by the fire. After a while Ma asked why Pa didn't play the fiddle, and he said, "I don't seem to have the heart to, Caroline."

After a longer while, Ma suddenly stood up.

"I'm going to hang up your stockings girls," she said. "Maybe something will happen."

Laura's heart jumped. But then she thought again of the creek and she knew nothing could happen.

Ma took one of Mary's clean stockings and one of Laura's and she hung them from the mantelshelf, on either side of the fireplace. Laura and Mary watched her over the edge of the bed-covers.

"Now go to sleep." Ma said, kissing them good night. "Morning will come quicker if you're asleep."

She sat down again by the fire and Laura almost went to sleep. She woke up a little when she heard Pa say. "You've only made it worse, Caroline." And she thought she heard Ma say: "No, Charles. There's the white sugar." But perhaps she was dreaming.

Then she heard Jack growl savagely. The doorlatch rattled and someone said, "Ingalls!Ingalls!" Pa was stirring up the fire, and when he opened the door Laura saw that it was morning. The outdoors was grey.

"Great fish-hooks, Edwards! Come in, man! What's hapened?" Pa exclaimed.

Laura saw the stockings limply dangling, and she scrooged her

44

shut eyes into the pillow. She heard Pa piling wood on the fire, and she heard Mr Edwards say he had carried his clothes on his head when he swam the creek. His teeth rattled and his voice quivered. He would be all right, he said, as soon as he got warm.

"It was too big a risk, Edwards," Pa said. "We're glad you're here, but that was too big a risk for a Christmas dinner."

"Your little ones had to have a Christmas," Mr Edwards replied. No creek could stop me, after I fetched them their gifts from Independence."

Laura sat straight up in bed. "Did you see Santa Claus?" she shouted.

"I sure did," Mr Edwards said.

"Where? When? What did he look like? What did he say? Did he really give you something for us?" Mary and Laura cried.

"Wait, wait a minute!" Mr Edwards laughed. And Ma said she would put the presents in the stockings, as Santa Claus intended. She said they mustn't look.

Mr Edwards came and sat on the floor by their bed, and he answered every question they asked him. They honestly tried not to look at Ma, and they didn't quite see what she was doing.

When he saw the creek rising, Mr Edwards said, he had known that Santa Claus could not get across it. ("But you crossed it," Laura said. "Yes," Mr Edwards replied, "but Santa Claus is too old and fat. He couldn't make it, where a long, lean razor-back like me could do so.") And Mr Edwards reasoned that if Santa Claus couldn't cross the creek, likely he would come no farther south than Independence. Why should he come forty miles across the prairie, only to be turned back? Of course he wouldn't do that!

So Mr Edwards had walked to Independence. ("In the rain?" Mary asked. Mr Edwards said he wore his rubber coat.) And there, coming down the street in Independence, he had met Santa Claus. ("In the daytime?" Laura asked. She hadn't thought that anyone could see Santa Claus in the daytime. No, Mr Edwards said; it was night, but light shone out across the street from the saloons.)

Well, the first thing Santa Claus said was. "Hello, Edwards!" ("Did he know you?" Mary asked, and Laura asked, "How did you know he was really Santa Claus?" Mr Edwards said that Santa Claus knew everybody. And he had recognised Santa at once by his whiskers. Santa Claus had the longest, thickest whitest set of whiskers west of the Mississippi.)

So Santa Claus said, "Hello, Edwards! Last time I saw you you were sleeping on a corn-shuck bed in Tennessee." And Mr Edwards well remembered the little pair of red-yarn mittens that Santa Claus had left for him that time.

Then Santa Claus said: "I understand you're living now down along the Verdigris River. Have you ever met up, down yonder, with two little young girls named Mary and Laura?"

"I surely am acquainted with them," Mr Edwards replied.

"It rests heavy on my mind," said Santa Claus. "They are both of them sweet, pretty, good little young things, and I know they are expecting me. I surely do hate to disappoint two good little girls like them. Yet with the water up the way it is, I can't ever make it across the creek. I can figure no way whatsoever to get to their cabin this year. Edwards, would you do me a favour to fetch them their gifts this one time?"

"I'll do that, and with pleasure," Mr Edwards told him.

Then Santa Claus and Mr Edwards stepped across the street to the hitching-posts where the pack-mule was tied. ("Didn't he have his reindeer?" Laura asked. "You know he couldn't," Mary said. "There isn't any snow." "Exactly," said Mr Edwards, Santa Claus travelled with a pack-mule in the south-west.)

And Santa Claus uncinched the pack and looked through it, and he took out the presents for Mary and Laura.

"Oh, what are they?" Laura cried; but Mary asked, "Then what did he do?"

Then he shook hands with Mr Edwards, and he swung up on his fine bay horse. Santa Claus rode well, for a man of his weight and build. And he tucked his long, white whiskers under his bandana. "So long, Edwards," he said, and he rode away on the Fort Dodge trail, leading his pack-mule and whistling.

Laura and Mary were silent an instant, thinking of that.

Then Ma said. "You may look now girls."

Something was shining bright in the top of Laura's stocking. She squealed and jumped out of bed. So did Mary, but Laura beat her to the fireplace. And the shining thing was a glittering new tin cup.

Mary had one exactly like it.

These new tin cups were their very own. Now they each had a cup to drink out of. Laura jumped up and down and shouted and laughed, but Mary stood still and looked with shining eyes at her own tin cup.

Then they plunged their hands into the stockings again. And they pulled out two long, long sticks of candy. It was peppermint candy, striped red and white. They looked and looked at the beautiful candy, and Laura licked her stick, just one lick. But Mary was not so greedy. She didn't take even one lick of her stick.

Those stockings weren't empty yet. Mary and Laura pulled out two small packages. They unwrapped them, and each found a little heart-shaped cake. Over their delicate brown tops was sprinkled white sugar. The sparkling grains lay like tiny drifts of snow.

The cakes were too pretty to eat. Mary and Laura just looked at them. But at last Laura turned hers over, and she nibbled a tiny nibble from underneath, where it wouldn't show. And the inside of that little cake was white!

It had been made of pure white flour, and sweetened with white sugar.

Laura and Mary never would have looked in their stockings again. The cups and the cakes and the candy were almost too much. They were too happy to speak. But Ma asked if they were sure the stockings were empty.

Then they put their arms down inside them, to make sure.

And in the very toe of each stocking was a shining bright, new penny!

They had never even thought of such a thing as having a penny. Think of having a whole penny for your very own. Think of having a cup and a cake and a stick of candy *and* a penny.

There never had been such a Christmas.

Now, of course, right away Laura and Mary should have thanked Mr Edwards for bringing those lovely presents all the way from Independence. But they had forgotten all about Mr Edwards. They had even forgotten Santa Claus. In a minute they would have remembered, but before they did, Ma said gently, "Aren't you going to thank Mr Edwards?"

"Oh, thank you, Mr Edwards! Thank you!" they said, and they meant it with all their hearts, Pa shook Mr Edwards' hand, too, and shook it again. Pa and Ma and Mr Edwards acted as if they were almost crying, Laura didn't know why. So she gazed again at her beautiful presents.

She looked up again when Ma gasped. And Mr Edwards was taking sweet potatoes out of his pockets. He said they had helped to balance the package on his head when he swam across the creek. He thought Pa and Ma might like them, with the Christmas turkey.

There were nine sweet potatoes. Mr Edwards had brought them all the way from town, too. It was just too much. Pa said so. "It's too much, Edwards," he said. They never could thank him enough.

Mary and Laura were much too excited to eat breakfast. They drank the milk from their shining new cups, but they could not swallow the rabbit stew and cornmeal mush.

"Don't make them, Charles," Ma said, "it will soon be dinner time."

For Christmas dinner there was the tender, juicy, roasted turkey. There were the sweet potatoes, baked in the ashes and carefully wiped so that you could eat the good skins, too. There was a loaf of salt-rising bread made from the last of the white flour.

And after all that there were stewed dried blackberries and little cakes. But these little cakes were made with brown sugar and they did not have white sugar sprinkled over their tops.

Then Pa and Ma and Mr Edwards sat by the fire and talked about Christmas times back in Tennessee and up north in the Big Woods. But Mary and Laura looked at their beautiful cakes and played with their pennies and drank water out of their new cups. And little by little they licked and sucked their sticks of candy, till each stick was sharp-pointed on one end.

That was a happy Christmas.

Christmas Tea

It's usually a good idea to go out for a walk at some stage on Christmas afternoon so as to ensure that everyone has got rid of that full feeling that comes from a huge lunch. Christmas afternoon is a lovely time to be out and about: you can see the Christmas lights glittering from the trees in different windows as the dark begins to fall, and you can wish a "Merry Christmas" to anyone you meet. You could go "cribbing"—visit a couple of churches to see and admire the crib, pray for a moment, and leave a small donation.

Christmas tea is best served late and informally: buttered toast and cold ham. Christmas cake and a Christmas log, cups of a special brew of tea like Earl Grey.

A Christmas Log

The "Yuletide Log" is a very old English tradition associated with Christmas. In the days when an open fireplace was the main way of heating a house, a great log would be brought in on Christmas Eve, and lit amid great ceremony from the charred embers of the previous year's log which had been saved from the occasion. Once lit, the Yule Log had to be kept alight for the whole of the Christmas season, being damped down at night but fanned into flame again next day. In some areas, it was a tradition that for as long as the log burned, the servants of the house would have wine and ale with their meals: you can imagine that there were great efforts to ensure that it burned as long and as slowly as possible!

You can make an edible "Yule Log" to commemorate the old custom. Take a chocolate swiss roll cake, cover it with chocolate icing, and draw lines down it with a fork so that it looks like tree bark. Sprinkle some white icing-sugar on top for snow. Add a bit of holly, or a little model of a robin.

Another idea, which I got from Australia, is for a ginger log. Christmas is celebrated in the middle of the summer in Australia— but people mostly still tend to eat turkey and Christmas pudding! The early pioneers there, missing "Home" terribly at this season, used to cook the whole hot meal and eat it with great ceremony. Nowadays, the turkey is mostly served cold with salad and there are various recipes for cold versions of Christmas pudding. Families picnic on the beach or by a river for coolness. But they still decorate their houses, and have Christmas trees, and the children hang up stockings (Santa Claus comes hurtling across Australia, they are told, on a cart drawn by six white kangaroos or "boomers".)

This "ginger log" is not a particularly Christmassy dish in Australia, but I thought it could suitably become one. The recipe comes from a delightful Australian relation who compiled a most useful cookery book called *Really Easy but Delicious.*

Ginger Log

1 packet ginger nut biscuits
half a pint of stiffly whipped cream
1 cup finely chopped crystallised ginger

Sandwich together a packet of ginger nut biscuits with whipped cream. Cover log with more cream and roll loosely in foil. (It looks a ghastly mess but don't worry.)

Leave in fridge for 24 hours.

Unroll, cover with more cream and sprinkle with crystallised ginger. It should look like a white log and be served sliced

Christmas Around the World

An enjoyable talking-point at Christmas is how it is celebrated around the globe. A friend who works for an international Christian charity describes spending a Christmas in central Africa:

"We arrived in time for midnight Mass, which the priest who had come with me celebrated. We were at a convent. The nuns had been practising for weeks with some special music for this Mass. They do not have a regular priest and see a visiting one only fairly rarely. The music was superb. There was a tremendous air of a special occasion: the excitement was tangible all the time.

After Mass we went into the main room of the convent. These nuns are very poor. They are really living—along with the other people of the district—at subsistence level. And do you know what they had for their Christmas feast? Peanuts. That's all. Just peanuts. They were set out in small dishes along the table. But the nuns had arranged a whole programme of music and dancing and singing for us. They danced in a traditional tribal style, and sang beautifully, and we were expected to join in. Being embarrassed and European, we felt stiff and shy. I'm not used to stamping about and chanting and singing in the middle of the night. But these sisters celebrated Christmas with a joy that I've not seen in most places in the Western world: a genuine enthusiasm because Christ was born and the Christian message is beautiful. They have absolutely nothing in material terms: they are desperately poor. But for them, it was enough at Christmas that they had had a special Mass, and some guests, and a chance to take a little holiday and be merry together."

I thought of this during a conversation I had after one Christmas with some very well-to-do people within the diplomatic community of a big European city. "Oh, I loathe Christmas", one of them said crossly, tired of the subject. "All that eating, and all those ghastly parties. I get more sick of it each year. It doesn't mean anything at all. Why do we go on bothering with it? I'm always glad when it's over and we can all give up pretending enjoyment."

No wonder Our Lord feels happiest among the poor.

Christmastide

Christmas is emphatically *not* over with bedtime on Christmas Day. It's only just begun: there are twelve days of celebration and no modern commercial pressure should prevent our enjoying to the full this holiest of feasts. Most schools will still be on holiday—pantomimes are in full swing. *Now* is the time for all our parties and family visits and the merrymaking for which Advent was a preparation.

Boxing Day—St Stephen's Day—December 26

> *Give us grace, Lord, to practise what we worship.*
> *Teach us to love our enemies*
>   *as we keep the feast of St Stephen,*
> *Who prayed even for the men who stoned him to death.*
> *We make our prayer through Our Lord.*
> > *(from The Divine Office)*

Boxing Day refers to the custom of giving Christmas "boxes"—presents to the people who have worked for us during the year. It proves that our ancestors didn't hold with all this nonsense of celebrating Christmas halfway through Advent. Their boxes were distributed on December 26, which as far as they were concerned was in the very heart of Christmastide.

You will probably have distributed your Christmas boxes already, if you do so at all, to the dustmen and the newspaper boy who suddenly appeared on your doorstep and wished you a "Merry Christmas" on December 18th or 19th. They were expecting money: one way to make it all a bit more Christmassy is to put the cash into envelopes decorated with Christmas seals and, if you've got the courage, to say when you hand them over that they are Christmas Boxes and ought properly to be opened on Boxing Day.

Boxing Day in Britain is usually a visiting-relations day, and boxes will be very much in evidence as visiting means more presents being exchanged. It is also, ideally, an outdoor day—a day or a good long walk to get rid of the overfed feeling and perhaps a visit to a nice Christmassy pub.

Glüwein

The name literally means "Glow-wine" (you pronounce it "gloo-vine") and it's a delicious spicy hot wine that really does give you a glow inside. It's superb after a Boxing Day walk and is nice to offer visitors emerging cramped and cold from a car after a long journey, too. Germans have been enjoying it for generations, especially after skating, snowballing, or tobogganing.

First stick about a dozen cloves each into a lemon and an orange (children can help with doing this) and put them into the oven on a very low heat, to warm.

Now pour two bottles of red wine into a saucepan, and add four tablespoons of sugar, three cloves, some orange and lemon slices, and a stick of cinnamon. Put in the orange and lemon from the oven when they have been warmed through. Heat it all up, and serve!

Ideas for Boxing Day

December 26, like December 25, *shouldn't* be a television day. One family I know always has an outdoor picnic on Boxing Day—hot soup in flasks, mince pies, plenty to drink. Why not? Drive out with friends to a nice area, have a good long walk and then a picnic in the frosty air. It's exciting for children and beats stale cartoons on the TV hollow any time.

If, however, you're eating at home, the traditional thing is cold turkey and bubble-and-squeak. I *love* this dish—I'm sure I'm not alone in almost preferring it to the roast meal of the day before—and my Auntie Peggy makes a superb bubble-and-squeak for which she cooks the potatoes and sprouts specially, because there simply wouldn't be enough for everyone's enthusiastic appetites if it was only made from yesterday's leftovers.

The rest of yesterday's Christmas pudding is delicious fried in slices in butter, and served with whipped cream. But many people find that Boxing Day is the day when mince pies really come into their own, everyone having been too full to enjoy them the day before. Serve them hot and sugary with a great deal of cream and brandy butter.

Bubble and Squeak

You will need:

> *Potatoes (boiled, baked, roasted or mashed)*
> *boiled Brussels sprouts*
> *a little salt to taste*
> *fat for frying*

Simply mash the potatoes and sprouts together with some salt. It takes a bit of pounding, especially with roast potatoes, but it can be done. I expect an electric blender would do it beautifully, though I haven't tried. Then pile the mixture into the frying pan and fry quickly, turning frequently so that different bits of it get brown and crisp. Keep it in the oven until it's wanted. Serve it with the cold turkey, cold sausages, and some cranberry sauce.

St Stephen

Boxing Day is also St Stephen's Day. He was the first Christian martyr and has the privilege of a feast-day immediately next to Our Lord's birthday. He was chosen by the Twelve Apostles to be deacon, so that they could do their work as priests. He is the patron saint of altar servers. His story is told in the Acts of the Apostles:

"Stephen, a man richly blessed by God and full of power, performed great miracles and wonders among the people. But some men opposed him; they were members of the synagogue of the Free Men (as it was called), which had Jews from Cyrenia and Alexandria. They and other Jews from Cilicia and Asia started arguing with Stephen. But the Spirit gave Stephen such wisdom that when he spoke they could not resist him.

So they bribed some men to say, "We heard him speaking against Moses and against God!" In this way they stirred up the people, the elders, and the teachers of the Law. They came to Stephen, seized him, and took him before the Council. Then they brought in some men to tell lies about him. "This man", they said, "is always talking against our sacred temple and the Law of Moses. We heard him say that this Jesus of Nazareth will tear down the temple and change all the customs which have come down to us from Moses! All those sitting in the Council fixed their eyes on Stephen and saw that his face looked like the face of an angel.

The High Priest asked Stephen "Is this really so?" Stephen answered "Brothers and fathers! Listen to me!"

"Our ancestors had the tent of God's presence with them in the desert. It had been made as God had told Moses to make it, according to the pattern that Moses had been shown. Later on, our ancestors who received the tent from their fathers carried it with them when they went with Joshua and took over the land from the nations that God drove out before them. And it stayed there until the time of David. He won God's favour, and asked God to allow him to provide a house for the God of Jacob. But it was Solomon who built him a house.

"But the Most High God does not live in houses built by men; as the prophet says, Heaven is my throne, says the Lord. and earth is my footstool. What kind of house would you build for me? Where is the place for me to rest? Did not I myself make all these things?

"How stubborn you are! How heathen your hearts, how deaf you are to God's message! You are just like your ancestors: you too have always resisted the Holy Spirit! Was there any prophet that your ancestors did not persecute? They killed God's messengers, who long ago announced the coming of his righteous Servant. And now you have betrayed and murdered him. You are the ones who received God's law, that was handed down by angels—yet you have not obeyed it!"

As the members of the Council listened to Stephen they became furious and ground their teeth at him in anger. But Stephen, full of the Holy Spirit, looked up to heaven and saw God's glory, and Jesus standing at the right side of God. "Look!" he said "I see Heaven opened and the Son of Man standing at the right side of God!"

With a loud cry they covered their ears with their hands. Then they all rushed together at him at once, threw him out of the city and stoned him. The witnesses left their cloaks in charge of a young man named Saul. They kept on stoning Stephen as he called on the Lord, "Lord Jesus, receive my spirit!" He knelt down and cried out in a loud voice, "Lord! Do not remember this sin against them!" He said this and died.

And Saul approved of his murder."

(Acts 6: 8—7: 2a, 44—59)

The story of St Stephen ought to be told at some stage on St Stephen's Day. It's worth pointing out that in a month's time, January 25th, the Church will be celebrating the feast of the Conversion of St Paul: we've heard today how he kept guard on people's coats while they got on with the stoning of Stephen, but we can look ahead and remind ourselves that in due course *he* was going to be converted and end up a Christian saint, too. Perhaps it was Stephen's prayers while on the point of death that helped to bring about this miracle and so give the Church one of its greatest teachers whose letters are still read out to us Sunday by Sunday.

A St Stephen's Day Rhyme

In Ireland, children go from house to house on St Stephen's Day, dressed up and wearing masks. They carry decorated branches of holly, with colourful streamers hanging from them—like a Wassail branch (see under "Wassailing"). At every house they collect sweets and money, after chanting:

> *"The wren, the wren*
> *The king of all the birds*
> *St Stephen's Day, she was caught in the furze.*
> *Droleen, droleen [meaning 'Little wren, little wren']*
> *Where is your nest?*
> *Beside the bush that I love best*
> *Between the holly and the ivy tree*
> *Where all the birds will sing to me.*
>
> *Mr ... [neighbour's name] is a wealthy man*
> Right to his door we've brought the wren, ..."

I think that any neighbour who resists this call must be very hard-hearted.

St Wenceslaus

On the Feast of St Stephen, because of the famous and still-popular carol, we think also of St Wenceslaus. His story, along with that of Stephen, ought to be told today. And of course it's fun to sing the carol, with different people taking the parts of King and page-boy, and perhaps children also acting it out (afterwards you all enjoy some spiced wine and some food and think of King Wenceslaus and the page-boy and the beggar all enjoying their food together beside a roaring pine-log fire).

St Wenceslaus, Christian King by Peggy Moen

The traditional Christmas carol *Good King Wenceslaus* tells the legend of a ruler who sees a poor man gathering fuel on the Feast of St Stephen, the martyr, and, learning where he lives from a page, decides to bring him Christmas cheer.

55

Good King Wenceslaus looked out
On the feast of Stephen,
When the snow lay round about
Deep and crisp and even.
Brightly shone the moon that night,
Though the frost was cruel,
When a poor man came in sight
Gathering winter fuel.

"Hither, page, and stand by me
If thou know'st it, telling
Yonder peasant, who is he?
Where and what his dwelling?"
"Sir, he lives a good league hence,
Underneath the mountain,
Right against the forest fence,
By St Agnes Fountain".

"Bring me flesh and bring me wine
Bring me pine logs hither
Thou and I shall see him dine
When we bear them thither".
Page and monarch forth they went
Forth they went together
Though the rude wind's wild lament
And the bitter weather".

"Sir, the night is darker now,
And the wind blows stronger.
Fails my heart—I know not how—
I can go no longer."
"Mark my foorsteps, good my page
Tread thou in them boldly:
Thou shalt find the winter's rage
Frezze thy blood less coldly."

In his master's steps he trod
Where the snow lay dinted.
Heat was in the very sod
Which the saint had printed.
Therefore, Christian men, be sure,
Wealth or rank possessing,
Ye who now do bless the poor
Shall yourselves find blessing.

In reality, Wenceslaus, King and martyr of tenth-century Bohemia, suffered a far less carefree life than the carol's cheer suggests: his family was divided into Christian and pagan factions, and murder commonly was used to dispose of opponents. The tale of their struggles resembles a Gothic horror story, alleviated by the great sanctity of the Christian rulers. Wenceslaus' grandfather, Borivoy, converted to Christianity and his wife, St Ludmilla, soon followed him. Both were baptized by St Methodius. They made definite, though largely fruitless attempts to Christianize their realm; they did build a church in Prague. Ratislav, their son, also professed Christianity, but his wife, Drahomira, adhered to paganism.

Much of the strife developed from the fears of the pagan nobility over Wenceslaus' great piety, the result of his grandmother's loving and thorough guidance. When Ratislav died, Drahomira seized her opportunity, became regent, and shortly afterwards Ludmilla was strangled to death, possibly under her daughter-in-law's direction. Then began a persecution of the Church in Bohemia, marked by the regent's banning of instructions in the Christian Faith. Ludmilla had hoped to help Wenceslaus take over the throne for the sake of the position of the Church in Bohemia, but her death prevented these plans from taking place.

Wenceslaus spent much of his time at this period of intensive prayer and study, readying himself for the struggles ahead over the role of Christianity in his realm. His prayer life had its beginning and end in devotion to the blessed Sacrament. Among the cruelties and connivings of the pagan nobles, his devotional life kept him perfectly charitable and innocent.

Drahomira's reign ended when her son came of age. One of his first concerns was to restore the priests to their duties in Bohemia and all of his governing reflects genuinely Christian ideals. What gives the legend of the Christmas carol some credibility is his love of the poor, and his ruthless, unyielding policy of ending the injustices inflicted on them by the nobility.

With typical determination. Wenceslaus worked hard for reconciliation with the German king, Henry I (usually considered one of the Holy Roman Emperors, although he never received the imperial crown). This, too, increased his alienation from the nobility who did not care for Christian alliances. When King Henry, who greatly admired Wenceslaus' piety, asked him to request any favor he desired, he asked for a relic of St Vitus, so he could build a church in Prague. This project was completed eventually, but not in

Wenceslaus' lifetime. Only his unfulfilled desire to finish the church kept him from abdicating and entering a monastery.

His foreign policy always reflected his other-worldliness. An intriguing story of peaceful military encounter is told in Butler's *Lives of the Saints:* when all hope of reconciliation with an invading, nearby tribe ended, and two armies confronted each other on the battlefield. Wenceslaus suggested that he and Ratislas, the other prince, joust with each other and thus spare many innocent lives. Rastislas, well-armed with a javelin in contrast to Wenceslaus' short sword, prepared to end his opponent with a single thrust, but suddenly saw two angels shielding the saint, and overawed, cast down his arms.

Miraculous manouvres of this sort were unfortunately not impressive to the pagan nobility, who hoped for generally more aggressive tactics. Wenceslaus' deranged, pagan brother Boleslas, popular with the nobility, desired more territory than he already controlled. To achieve this end, he and some discontented noblemen conspired to murder Wenceslaus. Boleslas invited his brother to Stara Boleslav for an evening party in honour of the Feast of Sts. Cosmas and Damian. The following morning, Wenceslaus on his way to Mass met Boleslas and thanked him for his generous hospitality. Boleslas replied, "Yesterday I did my best to serve you fittingly, but this must be my service today," and stabbed him with the help of three other conspirators. Wenceslaus, falling at the church door, said, "Brother, may God forgive you."

The people of Bohemia immediately proclaimed Wenceslaus a martyr—some would dispute the title, since the motivation for his murder was more political than religious. Yet Christian influence over the way of governing was what alienated the nobility and gave Boleslas his support: to die in defence of that influence is certainly martyrdom.

The manner of Wenceslaus' death reflects the manner in which he lived: alone and persecuted, with closeness to the Blessed Sacrement his final solace. His sorrow in all of his life turned outwards to those, like the poor and the mistreated, who also suffered. Throughout all his misery all his actions show no trace of despair or gloom.

Legends of the saints, such as the tale of Wenceslaus in the carol, do not tell a complete fiction about some episode in their lives; usually it refers to a true instance slightly improved upon to point out a holy person's virtue. This is certainly the case with "Good King Wenceslaus"; the king possessed great charity and generosity in fact, even though the event described probably never took place. The great charity he actually brought to the midst of the pagan court makes him a perfect Christmas saint; as Christ brought light to the entire world when it was in darkness by being born in a cave, surrounded by only a handful of people, so Wenceslaus carried out his God-given task by bringing a solitary, yet joyous Christian presence to a hostile setting.

(With thanks to *The Wanderer Christmas Book*, USA)

Holy Innocents Day—December 28

A voice was heard on high of lamentation, of mourning, and weeping, of Rachel weeping for her children, and refusing to be comforted because they are not.

(Jer. 31:15)

On Holy Innocents Day—Childermas—we think of the babies slaughtered by Herod in his attempt to kill the Christ Child.

Apparently it is an old tradition in some places for children to be soundly spanked on this day to remind them of the sufferings of the Innocents! I'm not sure that this is an idea which will endear itself to the younger members of the family.

In some areas of Britain, Childermas Day was called "Cross Day" and was marked as a day of mourning. There was an old saying that whatever was begun on this day would never come to fulfilment: hence it was (and is) an unpopular day for marriages. But elsewhere it was hailed as a day on which children should be shown special honour, as if in reparation for the slaughter of the innocents. Hence it became a day of merriment and games, centred on the littlest ones.

In Holland, it is traditional for the tiniest children to dress up as elderly men and woman and totter down the street in a procession on this day, collecting sweets and little gifts of money as they go.

A friend who lived for a while in a Franciscan religious community recalls that on Innocents Day one of the younger friars would be elected "Innocent", replacing the Abbot for the day and having to preside at ceremonies and preach a sermon, with everyone paying him much respect.

Some people in modern Britain have seen a parallel between the killing of the Innocents long ago and the destruction of unborn children today by abortion. Wreaths of white flowers are sometimes laid at specially-constructed shrines, and outdoor carol services held.

This did Herod sore affray
And grievously bewilder
So he gave the word to slay
And slew the little childer
And slew the little childer.

(15th cent. tr. G.R. Woodward.)

St Thomas of Canterbury – December 29

St Thomas à Becket, martyred in his own Cathedral at Christmastide, is honoured at this season. Born in London in 1118, martyred at Canterbury on December 29, 1170, he is one of the best known of English saints. His conflict with his king, Henry II, was to foreshadow another conflict between another Thomas and another Henry, Thomas More and Henry VIII, several centuries later.

The *Penguin Dictionary of Saints* tells the story:

"Thomas Becket was born in Cheapside of well-to-do Norman parents, and given a good all-round education. About 1142 he entered the service of Archbishop Theopold of Canterbury, who sent him abroad to study canon law and in 1154 gave him deacon's orders and the archdeaconry of Canterbury: in 1155 King Henry II chose him to be the royal chancellor. Becket was on terms of intimate friendship with the king, and served him faithfully and well for seven years as statesman, diplomat and soldier, appearing outwardly as the court ecclesiastic of extravagant worldly tastes and brilliant abilities. But when in 1162 Thomas was appointed to the vacant see of Canterbury, he changed from being, as he himself put it, 'a patron of play-actors and a follower of hounds, to being a shepherd of souls'. He threw himself into the duties of his new office, was profuse in alms-giving, lived very austerely, and soon came into conflict with the king. Of many points at issue between them, a crucial one for the archbishop concerned the respective jurisdictions of church and state over clergymen convicted of crimes. The situation became embittered, the bishops were divided in their views, and in 1164, after a stormy royal council at Northampton, Becket fled secretly to France.

"It was six years before the king and the archbishop were apparently reconciled; but immediately Thomas arrived back in England, on 1 December, 1170, the quarrel broke out afresh, over certain bishops whom Becket had disciplined for infringing his see's prerogatives at the king's instigation. Henry, in Normandy, fell into a passion of rage and uttered reckless words which, probably not intentionally, were Thomas's death-warrant. Four knights hurried across the Channel and, in the early evening of December 29, killed the archbishop in a side chapel of his cathedral. Christendom was aghast; all over Western Europe Thomas was spontaneously acclaimed as a martyr, and in 1173 Pope Alexander III (who had not given him unqualified support) formally canonized him. For nearly 400 years St Thomas's shrine at Canterbury was one of the three or four greatest pilgrim resorts of Europe. There has been disagreement about the character of St Thomas Becket. Imperious and obstinate, ambitious and violent he was. But all the time there were indications of more exalted qualities, and the years of exile at Pontigny and Sens were a time of preparation for the final ordeal; his last words, as reported by one eye-witness, were a key to his ideals as archbishop: 'Willingly I die for the name of Jesus and in defence of the church'. The story of Thomas of Canterbury has attracted dramatists from Tennyson's *Becket* through T. S. Eliot's *Murder in the Cathedral* to Anouilh's play *Becket* which was made into a film in 1964."

New Year's Eve—St Sylvester

Few people need encouragement to celebrate New Year's Eve: it is fun to stay up until midnight, and then as the clock strikes to sing "Auld Lang Syne", to throw streamers, to exchange hugs and kisses, to toast the New Year.

There are dozens of local traditions associated with the New Year in various parts of the British Isles. Scotland is particularly rich in them, and most New Year's Eve parties these days have a vaguely Scottish flavour, with first-footing and whisky and a general merriment for Hogmanay.

New Year Traditions

The first person to set foot in the house in the New Year—and it's generally about half a minute after midnight when they do it—must on no account be a red-head, and must carry some coal. The coal is meant to be an assurance that the family will not want for warmth and fuel in the coming year. Some people used to put out on New Year's Eve a piece of coal, a piece of bread, and a silver sixpence (I suppose a newly polished shilling would do) and then bring them in after midnight or on New Year's morning, for the same reason. A red-head coming first into the house is a sign of arguments and strife in the year ahead. The best "first-footer" is someone dark-haired and dark-eyed.

Wassailing

An old tradition associated with the New Year is Wassailing: you go from house to house singing a song and offering God's blessing on the occupants for the forthcoming year, and being treated to bowls of spiced ale with apples and sugar in. The Wassail Cup was a large wooden bowl, often a family heirloom, which was used on these occasions. The word comes from the Saxon "Waes Hael!"—"Good health!" We still use the expression "hale and hearty"to describe some one in good health.

A Wassail Cup

Warm up 3 pints of beer, add one teaspoonsful of mixed spice, and four tablespoons of sugar, slice four peeled apples into the mixture, & stir until the sugar is dissolved. Serve from a large bowl, saying "God bless you and bring you good health in the year ahead" as you give each person a mugful. You could take some to the neighbours, too, carrying your Wassail-branch! Also, it is traditional to pour a little round the apple—trees in the garden, asking God's blessing on next year's fruit crop.

The Wassail Song

Here we come a-wassailing
Among the leaves so green
Here we come a-wandering
So fair to be seen:
Chorus:
Love and joy come to you
And to you your wassail too,
And God bless you and send you
A Happy New Year.
And God send you a Happy New Year.

62

We are not daily beggars
That beg from door to door
But we are neighbour's children,
Whom you have seen before. Chorus.

God bless the master of this house,
God bless the mistress too,
And all the little children
That round the table go. Chorus.

When you go wassailing, you carry a Wassail-branch. It might be fun for children to make one for New Year's Eve. It is an evergreen branch, tied to a tall stick (a broom-handle would do beautifully if you can detach it from the broom. Or a walking-stick might do). You decorate it as you would do a Christmas tree, with silvered baubles and oranges and tinsel and bits of ribbon: it's traditional to have red ribbons tied in big bows on it. Every child should have one of his own for the Wassailing. The ornaments need to be tied on very firmly or they will fall off during the walk.

St Sylvester

When we spent a New Year in Germany, we were baffled as to why they referred to New Year's Eve as "Sylvester". There were Sylvester dances, Sylvester parties, Sylvester discos, Sylvester cakes on sale, and boxes of fireworks for the Sylvester celebrations in all the shop windows.

Then we discovered that December 31st is the Feast of St Sylvester. He is a saint whom we seem conveniently to have forgotten in England, which is very silly because he was a most important figure in our Church history and in the formation of modern civilisation. He was elected Pope in the year 314 and ruled during the time of Constantine, the Great Roman Emperor who was responsible for making the Roman Empire into a Christian one. Constantine put an end to the persecution which Christians had been enduring, and his reign also brought great peace and stability to the peoples of the Empire.

St Sylvester was buried in Rome in the year 335.

Epiphany—Twelfth Night: January 6

For we have seen His star in the East
and have come to worship Him.
(Matthew 2.2)

On the feast of Epiphany—the word comes from the Greek for manifestation or appearance, and refers to the showing of God to man—we celebrate the day on which Our Lord was shown to a wider public, and in particular when the Wise Men from a far country came to worship Him.

In Britain, its old name is Twelfth Night: it is the final day of the twelve days of celebration that mark the Christmas feast. It is traditionally the day for taking down the Christmas decorations. It is a Holyday of the Church and a good day for a party. Shakespeare wrote a play in honour of Twelfth Night. The keynote of the feast is fun and joy: Christ is with us, He is among men, a Child who is to become our Saviour.

"We three kings of Orient are
Bearing gifts we traverse afar,
Field and fountain, moor and mountain
Following yonder star.
O star of wonder, star of night,
Star with royal beauty bright,
Westward leading, still proceeding,
Guide us to thy perfect light.

Born a king on Bethlehem plain,
Gold I bring to crown him again,
King for ever, ceasing never,
Over us all to reign.

Frankincense to offer have I
Incense owns a Deity nigh
Prayer and praising, all men raising
Worship Him, God most high.

Myrrh is mine, its bitter perfume,
Breaths a life of gathering gloom;
Sorrowing, sighing, bleeding, dying
Sealed in the stone-cold tomb.
(John Henry Hopkins 1822-1900)

Today the Three Kings, moving along towards the crib, have finally reached the manger. We could celebrate with a festival meal, crackers on the table, games. If the Christmas decorations are paper chains that we will not be keeping for next year, and the tree is not for planting, we could have a bonfire. We could sing all the carols that refer to the three Wise Men. We could act out a nativity play and tell the story from their point of view: their first sight of the star and their consulting with maps and charts, their choice of gifts (the carol "We three kings" helps to explain why they chose them. All the gifts were of symbolic significance to show Our Lord's sovereignty, divinity, and ultimate sacrifice), their meeting with Herod and their final foiling of him by the angel's warning so that they went home by a different route.

The story of the visit of the Magi comes in St Matthew's Gospel, chapter 2, and could usefully be read today, perhaps by the light of the Christmas tree: this is the last day on which we can enjoy the tree's lights and decorations. The Gospel account does not give us the names of the Wise Men, or even state categorically that there were three of them, but long tradition has given them the names of Kaspar, Melchior, and Balthasar.

The bodies of the three are said to lie in Cologne Cathedral, where there is a shrine to them! In Germany—and in Scandinavia—children dress up as "star singers" on January 6th: boys gather together in groups of three, and dress as the Three Kings, wearing crowns and cloaks. They carry a star on a tall stick, and go from house to house singing and collecting money. Sometimes the star is in the form of a lantern, with a candle inside. They then chalk up the initials of the three kings, and the date, above the door of the house (see "A House Blessing").

A Twelfth Night Party

January 6th is ideal for a party—it marks the final end of the Christmas season and makes a bright note in January, otherwise a cold and sometimes cheerless month. High points of the party could include the appearance of three "star singers", the reading of the story of the Three Kings, a galette and the arrival of "Befana" as described below, and of course the final plundering of the Christmas tree and distribution of its gifts and edibles. In Sweden, once the tree has been finally stripped of all its decorations, it is handed over to the children to be finally tossed out of the back door while they chant:

> *"Christmas has come to an end*
> *And the tree must go*
> *But next year once again*
> *We shall see our dear old friend*
> *For he has promised us so."*

It is also fun to sing—and perhaps to act out—the old song about the Twelve Days of Christmas.

> *On the first day of Christmas, my true love sent to me*
> *A partridge in a pear tree.*

> *On the second day of Christmas, my true love sent to me*
> *Two turtle doves*
> *And a partridge in a pear tree.*

> *On the third day of Christmas, my true love sent to me*
> *Three French hens*
> *Two turtle doves And a partridge in a pear tree.*

> *On the fourth day of Christmas, my true love sent to me*
> *Four colly birds*
> *Three French hens*
> *Two turtle doves*
> *And a partridge in a pear tree.*

> *On the fifth day of Christmas, my true love sent to me*
> *Five gold rings*
> *Four colly birds*
> *Three French hens*
> *Two turtle doves*
> *And a partridge in a pear tree*

> *On the sixth day of Christmas, my true love sent to me*
> *Six geese a-laying*
> *Five gold rings*
> *Four colly birds*

66

Three French hens
Two turtle doves
And a partridge in a pear tree.

On the seventh day of Christmas, my true love sent to me
Seven swans a-swimming
Six geese a-laying
Five gold rings
Four colly birds
Three French hens
Two turtle doves
And a partridge in a pear tree.

On the eighth day of Christmas, my true love sent to me
Eight maids a-milking
Seven swans a-swimming
Six geese a-laying
Five gold rings
Four colly birds
Three French hens
Two turtle doves
And a partridge in a pear tree

On the ninth day of Christmas, my true love sent to me
Nine drummers drumming
Eight maids a-milking
Seven swans a-swimming
Six geese a-laying
Five gold rings
Four colly birds
Three French hens
Two turtle doves
And a partridge in a pear tree.

On the tenth day of Christmas, my true love sent to me
Ten pipers piping
Nine drummers drumming
Eight maids a-milking
Seven swans a-swimming

Six geese a-laying
Five gold rings
Four colly birds
Three French hens
Two turtle doves
And a partridge in a pear tree.

On the eleventh day of Christmas, my true love sent to me
Eleven ladies dancing
Ten pipers piping
Nine drummers drumming
Eight maids a-milking
Seven swans a-swimming
Six geese a-laying
Five gold rings
Four colly birds
Three French hens
Two turtle doves
And a partridge in a pear tree.

On the twelfth day of Christmas, my true love sent to me
Twelve lords a-leaping
Eleven ladies dancing
Ten pipers piping
Nine drummers drumming
Eight maids a-milking
Seven swans a-swimming
Six geese a-laying
Five gold rings
Four colly birds
Three French hens
Two turtle doves
And a partridge in a pear tree.

An Explanation of the "Twelve Days of Christmas" Song

Mrs Iris Jones, of Muxton, Shropshire, sent me this fascinating explanation of the old song, saying "I found it on the back of an old letter which I was clearing out—I have passed it on to one or two people but thought that you may be able to bring it to a wider readership." I am happy to do so! According to Mrs Jones, the song was used as a form of catechism, from the 1550s to the 1820s, with children being taught their doctrine in this way:

1st Day My true Love—God
          Partridge—Jesus
          Pear Tree—Apple tree in the Garden of Eden
2   Turtle Doves—Old and New Testaments
3   French Hens—Faith, Hope, and Charity
4   Colly Birds—4 Gospels
5   Gold rings—1st 5 books of the Old Testament
6   Geese a-laying—6 days of Creation
7   Swans a-swimming—7 gifts of the Holy Spirit
8   Maids a-milking—8 Beatitudes
9   Ladies dancing—9 Fruits of the Holy Spirit (Gal 5:23)
10   Lords a-leaping—10 Commandments
11   Pipers piping—11 faithful disciples
12   Drummers drumming—12 points of belief in the
          Apostles' Creed.

For more information about the seven "gifts of the Holy Spirit" see the section on Pentecost.
The eight Beatitudes are:-

Blessed are the poor in spirit; for theirs is the kingdom of Heaven.
Blessed are the meek; for they shall inherit the earth.
Blessed are they that mourn; for they shall be comforted.
Blessed are they that hunger and thirst after righteousness for they shall have their fill.
Blessed are the merciful; for they shall obtain mercy.
Blessed are the pure of heart; for they shall see God.
Blessed are the peacemakers; for they shall be called Children of God.
Blessed are they that suffer persecution for My name's sake; for theirs is the Kingdom of Heaven.

The reference is to St. Matthew's Gospel, chapter five, the Sermon on the Mount

Galette du Rois

The French have a particularly enjoyable way of celebrating Epiphany, with the "Galette du Rois". Two pretty crowns are made of gold paper and set in the middle of the table. The Galette is a cake made of flaky pastry filled with marzipan. A dried bean is popped into the filling. When the cake is sliced, whoever gets the bean is King or Queen for the evening. They are ceremonially crowned with one of the golden crowns and they choose a consort of the opposite sex who is given the other crown. Everyone then drinks their health. Two portions of the cake are traditionally set aside, in the name of Jesus and of Mary His Mother, for the poor, "qui se rejouissant aussi en ce jour de triomphe du Roi humble et pauvre ... " You take them to elderly lonely neighbours. The King and Queen have the privilege of choosing the first games that are to be played after the meal.

Recipe for the Galette du Rois

Buy two half-pound packets of ready-made puff pastry, and one half-pound packet of marzipan (Alternatively, make your own marzipan out of ground almonds and egg-yolks according to your favourite recipe).

I was sent by a French cook a delightful little token for the galette—a small figure of a king. It might be fun to try to obtain one of these by asking around, or begging friends who visit France to get one from there—they are sold in France as Christmas pudding tokens are sold here.

Alternatively, use a dried bean—or any other token you like.

Cut two rounds out of the puff-pastry, one from each half-pound. Keep them cool in the 'fridge while you cut a similarly-sized round from the marzipan. You will need a well-floured pastry board for all of this.

The rounds should be the size of the cake you want, and should fit comfortably into your baking-dish—a flan dish is a good dish to use.

Now put in the first round of pastry, top it with the marzipan and press the king token into the marzipan somewhere. Then put on the top round of pastry. Brush with beaten egg or with milk, and bake in a hot oven until golden and crispy (about 15 minutes). Serve warm. My French cook friend tells me a sauterne is the right wine to serve with it!

Befana

The Italians enjoy themselves on January 6. For them, it has always traditionally been the day when Christmas gifts are exchanged. It is Befana—a corruption of the word Epiphany—and the festivities are presided over by a witch of that name. She is a sort of female Father Christmas, and arrives laden with presents.

Befana could make an appearance at your Twelfth Night party, in a witch's hat and costume, bringing a small gift for each guest. Or she could preside over another Italian custom—a sort of "lucky dip" in which people dip in a box and draw out parcels, some of which are blank, and some full.

One way to organise this Twelfth Night Dip is for every person to come to the party bearing three small parcels in honour of the Three Magi. Two of the parcels are blank and one has a small gift in it: something suitable for anyone at the party. Everyone then writes their names on pieces of paper and these are folded up and tossed into Befana's hat and stirred around vigorously. Each person then draws out a name, and whatever name you have drawn is then written on your three parcels. All the parcels are then thrown into a big box along with lots of bits of paper and straw (maybe this is where you can use up the Christmas decorations) and stirred around vigorously. The box should be a special festive one, properly decorated: children can have fun doing this the day before. It could be the linen basket or a big packing case (Army families could use an MFO box!) and is covered in Christmassy paper and trimmed with tinsel and glitter and ribbons. One by one you now take turns drawing parcels out of the box, watched by Befana, who superintends the proceedings and ensures fair play. When you draw out a parcel, you give it to the person whose name it bears, or open it yourself if it is yours. Of course it may be a blank one—general sympathy for your discomfiture. But everyone gets a gift in the end.

A House Blessing

The traditional way to end Epiphany is to bless the house. In some parts of Poland the priest visits all the houses of the parish, gathering a procession as he goes, blessing each home. Elsewhere in Europe various specific items are taken to church the day before Epiphany to be blessed: water, chalk, and incense. The blessed chalk is then used to write the initials of the three Wise Men up above the main door of the house, together with the year and a cross, like this: "19 K + M + B 92". Trooping outside with lanterns to sing a final carol and chalk up the initials of the Three Kings above the front door after a prayer of blessing might be a lovely way to finish your Twelfth Night party.

St Agnes—January 21

St Agnes Eve—Ah, bitter chill it was!
The owl, for all his feathers, was a—cold
The hare limp'd trembling through the frozen grass
And silent was the flock in woolly fold
(John Keats 1795—1821)

St Agnes was a young girl, martyred for her faith in the very early years of the Church, in the days of the Roman Empire. The approximate date of her death was 304 AD. She was a teenager—about 13 years of age. She refused to be given in marriage to a pagan, which would have meant her being forced to obey pagan laws and customs. Standing steadfast in her Christian faith and upholding her right to remain an unmarried virgin as she had chosen, she was publicly executed. Her name appears in the Church calendar from a very early date, and she has been honoured by generations of Christians. Her symbol is a lamb—the Latin word "Agnus" means a lamb. (Think of "Agnus Dei", the Lamb of God).

It is traditional for girls to invoke St Agnes in praying for a good husband. Some superstitions have built up around this. One tradition is that if an unmarried girl eats a hard-boiled egg *complete with shell* on the eve of St Agnes, she will see an image of her future husband in the mirror when she brushes her hair that night! Another tradition is to bake a dumb-cake: a fruit loaf, mixed and baked entirely in silence, and shared in silence with other young girls. If all maintain the silence, they too will see their future husbands in the mirror that night! It's probably all just a ruse to stop girls chattering.

It's fun for girls to talk and dream about their future husbands—and very right that they should pray about it (St Joseph and St Lucy, as mentioned elsewhere in this book, are also invoked for the same purpose!) But perhaps the story of St Agnes reminds us that the Church also honours unmarried women, and—uniquely amongst the

other religions of its day in the Roman Empire—upholds the right
of a woman to make a free choice. To remain a virgin, given to God
in freedom and service, is an honourable calling!

Candles at the end of Winter

A light to lighten the Gentiles
and the glory of your people, Israel.
(Luke 2:22—40)

Candlemas, the feast of the Presentation of Our Lord, celebrates
the day on which the infant Christ was taken by Mary His Mother
and St. Joseph to the Temple in Jerusalem where thanks would
be offered to God, according to the correct and ancient Jewish
custom. When Simeon, "an upright and devout man", well
advanced in years saw them he knew that this was the Child who
was the Messiah for which Israel and the world had been waiting.
He took the child in his arms and praised God and declared that
this Child would be a light to all the world, a light that would
enlighten pagans and give honour to the people of Israel from
whom He had sprung.

To commemorate what Simeon said, there are special candle
services in church—sometimes with a procession into the church
beforehand. These candles are blessed, and we can take them home
with us where they can be lit again for a family candlelight supper.
As the children light the candles for the meal and set them on the
table, they could repeat Simeon's Canticle (at the head of this
section). It is a nice idea for family prayers tonight to be round the
candlelit table instead of beside beds.

Some people used to hold that the Christmas decorations should
stay up until Candlemas—but that seems a very long time to me. I
should think the greenery must have been pretty dry and crisp by that
time and the crêpe paper dusty. But you could leave one tiny token
of holly somewhere, behind the kitchen clock or in some corner, to
be ceremoniously taken down and thrown away tonight.

There is an old saying—"Candlemas—candleless", meaning that
after Candlemas the days start getting longer, and we don't need
artificial light in the evenings. Spring is on the way, and we should
start enjoying it. Who will be the first in the family to see the first
snowdrop? The first shoots of crocus? The first tight green buds on
the trees?

Deep sleeps the Winter, cold, wet and grey:
Surely all the world is dead: Spring is far away.
Wait! the world shall waken: it is not dead, for lo
The Fair Maids of February stand in the snow!
(The Song of the Snowdrop Fairy)

St. Blaise's Day—February 3

This time of year is notorious for its coughs and colds. Almost every school has at least a handful of pupils absent, and classes are punctuated by snuffles and nose-blowing.

For those suffering from sore throats, the feastday of St Blaise comes exactly when it is most needed.

St Blaise is the patron saint of throat sufferers, and many churches hold a special ceremony in his honour today, in which candles are crossed beneath people's throats, and a special blessing imparted invoking the aid of St Blaise.

St Blaise was a bishop and a martyr. He was bishop of Sivas in Armenia in the fourth century. He is said to have miraculously healed a child who got a fish-bone stuck in its throat: some versions of the account say that this happened as he was being led through the city to martyrdom. He placed his hands on the child's throat, prayed, and the fish-bone came unstuck and the throat was healed and all was well.

The popularity of St Blaise seems to date from the eighth century, and he has been honoured in both the Eastern and Western churches since that time.

If your local church doesn't have a Blessing of Throats for St Blaise's day, ask why not. It is a charming ceremony, very enjoyable for children, and very comforting for mothers of coughing, sore-throated February families!

The symbol of St Blaise is the two crossed candles which are used in the throat-blessing ceremony.

Peace in our present life
and help towards the life to come:
this is the prayer, lord,
which your people offer on Saint Blaise's Day
with the support of his intercession
We make our prayer through our Lord.

St Valentine—February 14

American author Mary Reed Newland did some research on St Valentine's Day. February 14 is also the feast of Saints Cyril and Methodius—and very important saints they are, too, being the evangelists of Eastern Europe and joint patrons with St Benedict of Europe as a whole. It was St Cyril who produced the Cyrillic alphabet, a form of which is still used in Russia.

But in Britain February 14 is firmly fixed in the public mind as being linked with St Valentine, so it makes sense to find out why, and what Christian families can do to draw something creative and loving out of what is rapidly becoming a commercialised exercise in rather bad-taste sentimentality.

Mary Reed Newland writes in *The Year and Our Children:*

"There are three Saints Valentine listed in early martyrologies for the date of February 14. That their feasts should end up united to a celebration in honour of lovers seems to have been more an accident than a design, though there are interesting complications that conspired to make it so.

"Long ago the Romans celebrated the eve of their Lupercalia on February 14. This being a time of great festivity it is thought by some that the martyrdom of saints on this day was merely an added attraction to the pagan celebration. Still another possibility connects the Roman celebration in honour of Juno with this feast. The drawing of partners for the festival by maidens and youths often degenerated into extreme improprieties, and it is thought the desire to redeem the day suggested to Christians that they fix it as the date of the martyrs' feasts. Pope Gelasius appointed it an official feast in the fifth century and named St Valentine as the patron saint of lovers.

"Add to this the widespread belief during the Middle Ages that February 14 was the time of the mating birds; so it is no wonder that from it all evolved the custom of consecrating it to lovers as a proper day to exchange notes and poems and lovers' tokens. In Chaucer's *Parliament of Foules* there are lines spoken by *Nature* thus:

'Ye knowe wel, how on Saint Valentines day,
By my statute, and though my governance,
Ye do chese your makes, and after flie away ...'
The third line, I have discovered, translates 'Ye do choose your mates ...'

75

"The legend that one of the Saints Valentine left a note in his cell the morning of his execution, into which he 'cut curious devices' and wrote 'pious exhortations and assurances of love to the keeper's daughter, signing them "your Valentine" is of doubtful origin but accounts for the lacy paper and the signature which are (or used to be) part of all valentines. All this makes quite a pot-pourri of things which have contrived to make a great to-do about valentines, though only a little to do with the Valentines."

Mrs Newland suggests that St Valentine's day is a good day for talking to children about the reality of Christian love, and for stressing its beauty and strength in an age when it is so ignored and undervalued. It is a day, too, when we could pray for strength and courage to resist the pressures of the immoral society in which we live in Western Europe in the 1980s, and for the grace to pass on to others the full truth of the Church's teaching on these matters.

As anyone who has ever received one will testify, a genuine loving valentine is a *lovely* thing to have. Thousands and thousands of women have, tucked away in some box of treasures, a little card or token that thrilled them to the core when it first arrived on some distant February 14.

Although the commercial pressures on St Valentine's Day are to be deplored, it is surely good to see people sending loving messages to one another.

If children are to give valentines—to mothers and fathers and grandparents and so on—they should be home-made. It is very easy to make a heart-shape by drawing half a heart against the fold of a folded piece of paper, and then cutting round it and unfolding it. Mrs Newland suggests "Red construction paper, lace-paper doilies, wallpaper sample books, leftovers of wallpaper, flower seed catalogues in colour, cast-off magazines, water colours, poster paints, inks, glitter, floral stickers, white typing paper, ribbons, and many odds and ends may be used". She suggests making personalised valentines by putting on them the symbols of people's saints—a coat sliced in half for a Martin, a little flower for a Therese, small animals for a Frank or Francis, carpenter's tools for a Joseph, and so on.

You can buy heart-shaped cake tins of varying sizes fairly cheaply, and it might be fun to invest in one of these and have a pink and white frosted cake for tea on St Valentine's Day.

Shrovetide

Knick a knock upon the block
Flour and lard are very dear,
Please we come a-shroving here.
Your pan's hot and my pan's cold,
Hunger makes us shrovers bold:
Please to give us poor shrovers something here.
(an old begging rhyme for Pancake Day from *A Little Book of Old Rhymes*)

With the coming of Spring we look towards Lent and Easter. Lent begins with Shrovetide.

In Britain, Shrove Tuesday is "Pancake Day" and the Monday is still known in some districts as "Collop Monday". Both refer to the days when the Lenten fast was more strictly observed, and all the meat and eggs and cream had to be eaten up before the Lenten season began on Ash Wednesday. "Collops" means bits of meat, and pancakes are of course made lavishly with lots of eggs and cream and milk.

Obviously, with Lent coming up, Collop Monday and Pancake Day are times of fun and feasting before the solemn period sets in. In other parts of Europe, the celebrations are much more in evidence: it is Carnival time. The word "Carnival" comes from the Latin words for meat and for goodbye—it literally means "goodbye to meat" and the Carnival period was the time of hectic gaiety and good eating that preceded Lent. It is fun to allow something of the Carnival tradition into our own pancake celebrations.

I remember one Shrove Tuesday in Germany, passing the local open-air skating rink and seeing it crowded with children in carnival costumes—Mickey mouse masks, bright paper hats, faces painted with glitter or in stripes—making a tremendous noise. Both the Monday and the Tuesday—and often several days more—before Ash Wednesday are carnival time and the Germans call that Monday "Rose Montag". The tradition is strongest in southern Germany, but has spread north across the country. In recent times any suggestion of a Lent to follow has more or less been forgotten.

Alexander Howard writes in *Endless Cavalcade—A Diary of British Festivals and Customs, (Arthur Baker)* 1964. "Collop Monday was once a great day for merry-making associated with carnivals, and because of the numerous poems that used to be written for that day in honour of the reigning pagan spirit customary before penance, the day was also known as Poets Day. Until not very long ago Eton scholars composed valedictory verses to be recited on Collop Monday as part of a farewell gesture to hilarity, rich food and wine until the end of Lent."

Properly, part of the message of Carnival is that the fun can't last—it all has to stop when Lent begins. A sort of sad ending is an inevitable part of the authentic Carnival message: perhaps that is why the sad clown, the pathos of Harlequin, and the idea of all good things coming to an end— "The Carnival is Over" —is all part of the tradition.

It's cheating to try to have Carnival—or even pancakes on Pancake Day—without following it up with Lent. Of course we ought to enjoy ourselves—we'll get Lent off to a better start if we begin it feeling cheerful and grateful to God for the good things of life—but it's got to be an enjoyment that takes into account the real nature of the feast.

Shrovetide is about the forgiveness of sins—the word "to shrive" means to pronounce absolution. In pre-reformation England, people queued up at church to go to confession and be shriven as Lent began. A bell would be rung on Shrove Tuesday to beckon them to church: in some areas this is still rung but is called the "Pancake Bell". The Catholic Church still reminds everyone that they should go to confession during Lent, to be ready for Communion at Easter.

If you want a solemn thought on which to focus your mind as Shrovetide comes to its end, remember what happened as the Carnival ended in Dresden in Germany in 1945. It was the night of Shrove Tuesday when the Royal Air Force and the American air force struck this city which was crammed with refugees fleeing westwards from the advancing Soviet armies. Some families in the city had been trying to keep up old customs and many of the dead children's bodies recovered after the bombing raid were in carnival costumes. In the firestorm which followed the saturation bombing over 160,000 people were killed. It was indeed Ash Wednesday in every sense. The whole of the city centre, with its medieval buildings and unique works of art, was gutted and destroyed, with shimmering ashes and grey stumps left as memorials. Today, in the new town which stands on the site, every year on the anniversary of the raid church bells ring out solemnly in commemoration. The bombing of Dresden serves to remind us that even when people are fighting a war on the right side they can do wicked things.

Pancakes

> *2 eggs*
> *4 ozs wholemeal flour*
> *one pint of creamy milk*
> *a good pinch of salt*
> *you can multiply the ingredients as you need for the numbers of people.*

Mix all these together to form a smooth batter. Heat a very small amount of fat in the frying pan, pour in a little of the batter, swirl it round until it covers the bottom of the pan, and fry the first pancake. You may find this first one sticks a bit and is less successful than the others will be. You will need the pan very hot.

Everyone who wants to do so should be allowed to take his turn at tossing his own pancake. The object of tossing, of course, is to make sure it is cooked on both sides. It is no mean feat to flip over a half-cooked pancake by tossing it into the air: some people get the knack straight away and some never make it happen properly.

Pancakes are good with lemon and brown sugar, or with golden syrup. I personally like them with raspberry sauce and whipped cream.

Raspberry Sauce

> *Raspberry jam*
> *water*

Simply warm up the jam in a saucepan, and thin it out with the water until it is the right consistency for pouring. Keep it warm in the oven in a jug until it is needed.

A Pancake Race

It is fun to run a pancake race on Shrove Tuesday, if you can get a few families together. This is an event for mothers. It is a tradition in some villages in England.

Every woman taking part must wear a headscarf and an apron. She must bring along a frying pan with a half-cooked pancake in it. Better still, you could provide the batter mixture and dish it out into the heated pans just before the ladies line up for the race.

They line up along the starting line, and set off when a whistle or bell is sounded. Before reaching their destination, each must toss the pancake three times (in honour of the Trinity). Failure to do so means disqualification. The winner is the first home with the pancake tossed three times and still in the pan.

The winner should get a suitable prize (or may be you could even have a frying-pan as a trophy, that went from household to household with different winners over the years?) and the event should finish with pancakes all round and much festive munching.

A Pancake Supper for Mardi Gras

It is fun to have a proper Mardi Gras celebration on the eve of Lent. Of course the main food on offer will be pancakes. You start by serving savoury ones, and then go on to sweet fillings. Suggestions for savoury fillings for pancakes are:

Snipped up pieces of bacon (collops!) and mushrooms mixed together and fried
Mushrooms in a creamy sauce
Shrimps or other shellfish in a creamy sauce
Slices of avocado pear
Minced chicken in white sauce
Cottage cheese with chives, or with pineapple
Grated cheese and fried snippets of bacon mixed together
Fried tomatoes and bacon.

All guests should bring a bottle to the pancake party—or some other contribution to the feast. People should be invited to help make—and toss—the pancakes.

Doughnuts are another traditional pre-Lenten treat—presumably because, like pancakes, they are a good way of eating up all the fat and eggs. They could be on the menu for your Mardi Gras party. So could party hats, streamers, masks, and any Carnival paraphernalia you can find.

The party should end promptly at midnight. One family I know even has a tradition of doing all the washing-up and tidying away in complete silence, or at least subdued voices, because once midnight has struck the Carnival is over and Lent has begun. It's traditional to sweep away the last traces of carnival fun with a last burst of noise and merriment just before midnight strikes, perhaps forming a sort of conga-dance for this purpose.

80

Lent

Ash Wednesday

Ashes are a very ancient symbol of mourning and repentance. A very old tradition has penitents going about wearing "sackcloth and ashes".

Ashes are distributed in churches on Ash Wednesday, the first day of Lent. The priest dips his thumb in a small dish of ashes—made by burning the palms from the previous year's Palm Sunday—and then makes a cross with this thumb on a person's forehead, saying "Remember, man, that thou art dust, and into dust thou shalt return" or some other formula such as "Repent, and believe in the Gospel".

In the Catholic Church, Ash Wednesday, together with Good Friday, is a day of fasting and abstinence. This means that only one main meal (plus perhaps two light snacks as necessary) may be eaten, and no meat.

You will sometimes see, as you go about a town on Ash Wednesday, people with the distinctive mark of ashes on their foreheads.

Lenten Kedgeree

This is a special form of kedgeree that doesn't include eggs. It's extremely cheap to make, and the money that you save can go as Lenten Alms to whatever charity you have chosen to support this year.

For two people (and you can multiply the amounts as necessary):

One tin of sardines
3 cups of brown rice
a teaspoonful of mixed herbs
salt
one onion

Slice and fry the onion. Put the rice on to boil with a little salt. Remove the backbones from the sardines, and then put the fish, plus its oil, into a big mixing bowl. Chop it about with a fork and stir in

81

the mixed herbs and a good pinch of salt. Add the fried onions, and then the rice when it is cooked. Mix very thoroughly indeed. Put to heat through in the oven. Serve with a green salad, or with peas or tomatoes.

Many families find that it is best to serve the main meal for Ash Wednesday in the evening. This will be the first of your special Lenten meals, so it is nice to do something a little bit different to mark the occasion. One family I know has a special Grace for Lent which they only use during this season:

"Bless this food
Bless those who have prepared it
And give food to the hungry.
Amen."

Macaroni Cheese (my mother's recipe)

For two people (multiply as necessary):

Two and a half cups of macaroni
one pint milk
¼lb. Cheddar cheese
one large onion
one oz. butter
one oz. flour (I use wholemeal flour)
two tomatoes
for topping: generous cupful of grated cheese and breadcrumbs

Melt the butter, stir in the flour and add the milk and stir until the mixture is creamy. Bring to the boil very slowly to thicken. Grate the cheese and add it. Set on one side. Boil the macaroni with a pinch of salt until soft. Slice and fry the onions.

Lay the onions at the bottom of an ovenproof dish, put the macaroni on top and pour the cheese sauce over it. Stir so that all the macaroni is well covered by the cheese mixture. Sprinkle the grated cheese and breadcrumbs on the top. Heat through very thoroughly in the oven until the top is brown and golden. Just before serving, slice tomatoes on top in a ring round the edge.

Vegetable Casserole

You will need:

*Potatoes (allow at least two per person, more if you know their
appetites)*
carrots
lentils (half a cup per person)
split peas
celery
mushrooms
salt
dried herbs
stock

The potatoes taste better if they are left unpeeled (though
thoroughly scrubbed of course, and with any nasty-looking bits cut
out). Peel and chop all the other vegetables, not too small. Chop the
potatoes into quarters.

Then simply place them all, except for the mushrooms, in a big
casserole dish and cover with the stock (you can use stock made from
boiling up the remains of a joint—or do what I do and use stock cubes,
made up as directed on the packet), adding a generous helping of herbs
and a good couple of pinches of salt (later, when you taste it, you may
find you want more salt: it varies). Cook very slowly indeed in a
moderate oven. Add the mushrooms only when everything else is
cooked as they will spoil if cooked for too long. If you want the dish
completely meatless, you could make the stock from Marmite.

You may now like the stock thickened, or you may find the lentils
and peas have thickened it enough already. To thicken it, melt some
fat, add flour and mix it to a smooth paste, and then pour off some
of the stock from the casserole and add this to the flour mixture. Stir
and cook until it thickens, then pour it into the casserole and stir it
all together. Reheat for at least a further quarter of an hour before
serving.

Rabbi Lionel Blue's Excellent Vegetable Pie

Friends tried out this recipe one Good Friday after it had been
published in the *Universe* newspaper, and enthused about it so much
that now it's a standard family dish. With thanks to Rabbi Blue and
the *Universe* for allowing me to reprint it:

You start by making one pound of shortcrust pastry, with which you line an eight-inch pie dish: the sort with a loose bottom. Then "fill it with a layer of thinly-sliced swede, then a layer of thinly sliced potatoes, and then a layer of chopped onions. Cut up a quarter of a pound of thick mushrooms roughly and put them on top. Salt and pepper each layer before adding the next.

"Finally, cover and close the pie with the rest of the pastry. Crimp the edges and make two or three holes for steam. Paint the top with beaten egg yolk.

"Bake it at 350 degrees (Gas 4) for 90 minutes, or until the outside is dark gold and inside is cooked (test it with a knife)."

Vegetable Cream Pie (my own recipe)

You will need:

> *Potatoes (two per person)*
> *leeks (one per two people)*
> *an onion*
> *carrots (two per person)*
> *cauliflower*
> *broad beans*
> *a white sauce (I make mine with wholemeal, not white, flour)*
> *nutmeg*
> *some grated cheese*

Scrub and thinly slice the potatoes. Peel and chop the other vegetables. Grease a large oblong casserole dish and put a pie-crust raiser or a tall inverted egg-cup in the middle. Into the dish, put a layer of potatoes, then a layer of other vegetables, then more potatoes, and so on until all are used up. Sprinkle each layer with a little salt.

Make up some white sauce—sufficient to cover all the vegetables. Add to it some grated nutmeg (about half a teaspoonful to one pint of sauce) and a little grated cheese, and some salt. Pour the finished sauce over the vegetables and give the casserole a little jiggle to make sure it is evenly spread. Cook for two hours in a very low oven, or until the potatoes are soft and you can put a knife through easily and touch the bottom. Then cover the dish with pastry, return to a warmer oven and cook until it is brown, brushing the pastry first with milk to make the top glossy.

A Lenten Chart

Traditionally, Lent lasts forty days—the forty days that Christ spent in the wilderness, fasting and preparing for His public ministry.

These forty days exclude the Sundays of Lent. On Sundays, you can give yourself a bit of a break from any self-imposed penance you may have for this season. This is particularly so on the Fourth Sunday of Lent, Laetare Sunday, which is also known as Mothering Sunday.

For children, a Lenten Chart is a way of honouring Lent. This is an idea that I remember from my junior school.

You will need:

A large sheet of white cardboard or stiff paper, approx. 1 ft by 18 inches—or bigger if you like
felt tip crayons, or paints, a ruler and a pencil
some sheets of gummed paper, stars or squares in different colours
a ball-point pensome gold paint

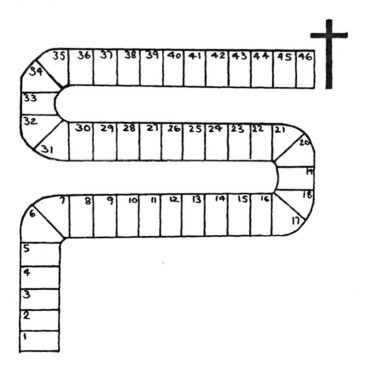

From the bottom of the page to the top draw a long wide snaky path like this, leaving a clear two inches at the top, at which you draw a large cross.

Now mark it off with a ruler into 46 different squares, like this— one square for each of the days in Lent (40 ordinary days and 6 Sundays).

This path marks Our Lord's route to Calvary. The forty squares are the forty days of Lent. At the top draw a large plain cross, using your ruler.

Now in each square, in very tiny lettering, print the special offering that is to be made to God that day. Some ideas to start you off:

"Today I will:

> read a story from the Bible about Jesus;
> eat no sweets;
> learn a bit of a psalm to recite;
> do a secret good turn to someone;
> watch no TV;
> not complain about *anything*;
> pray for Christians in countries where they
> are persecuted".

The point is to have a mixture: some acts of really quite difficult self-denial, some things that are enjoyable but require a little extra effort. You can of course repeat some ideas several times. Some squares could be left blank for a child to fill in with his own ideas.

You may need to explain to children that an act of self-denial, such as not eating sweets or watching TV doesn't mean that sweets or TV are wrong in themselves. It's simply a way of showing God how much we love Him, of thanking Him for all His gifts and learning to appreciate them more, and of understanding the use of our own willpower. Actually, most children have worked this one out for themselves and understand it better than some adults.

It is NOT a good idea to suggest things that look too pointed, or to refer in any way to any child's particular fault! That's just being mean. The whole them must be general. You can make identical charts by simply making one and getting it photocopied: this gives a professional appearance.

As each action is completed, the child covers up that day's square with a sticky-backed star or square. It's nice to have a purple square for Ash Wednesday: the action for that day should be "Today I will start Lent by receiving ashes". The square for Good Friday should be black, and the one for Laetare Sunday pink. The Laetare square should simply say "Laetare. Fourth Sunday of Lent. Today we rejoice!" All the other Sundays should say "1st Sunday of Lent", "2nd Sunday of Lent", etc., and not include any particular suggested activity: the child simply covers up the square after he has been to church.

On Good Friday, the children can decorate the sides of the chart with pictures depicting Our Lord carrying His Cross—perhaps even small scenes depicting the 14 Stations of the Cross.

On Holy Saturday night, after they are asleep, you paint along the edges of the path in gold, paint the cross at the top in gold, and add "Alleluia!" or "Happy Easter!" and the child's name, and any other trimmings you like, before pinning the chart back where it has hung all Lent. See how long it takes them to notice what's happened!

An important point: The whole effect and satisfaction of the chart is lost if grown-ups say pointedly "I thought you were going to keep your temper today!" or whatever. The idea is to make Lent a personal pilgrimage with Christ, *not* a source of nagging!

PS: Grown-ups could have charts, too, if they liked.

Mothering Sunday

On Mothering Sunday, above all other,
Every child should dine with its mother.
(from *A Little Book of Old Rhymes*)

Mothering Sunday is the fourth Sunday in Lent—Laetare Sunday. The "Laetare" comes from the Latin words at the Opening Prayer of this Sunday's Mass: "Laetare Jerusalem!", "Rejoice, Jerusalem!" We take a break from the gloom of Lent, and remember that Easter is on the way.

The tradition of the Fourth Sunday of Lent as Mothering Sunday goes back a long, long way.

The Romans honoured their goddess of motherhood in the Spring with the feast of Matronalia. Small cakes—made of a special extra-fine white flour known as *simila*—were baked and offered to her shrine.

When the Christian Church started to grow in different parts of the Roman Empire—including Britain—the Christians naturally incorporated the old customs into the new Gospel message. On the feast of Matronalia they honoured Mother Church, spiritual mother of all Christians everywhere.

The Entrance Antiphon for today's Mass in Catholic churches still echoes that theme of motherhood: "Rejoice, Jerusalem! Be glad for her, you who love her; rejoice with her, you who mourned for her, and you will find contentment at her consoling breasts." (ICEL tr.)

Some Church of England parishes still keep up the old custom of "clypping the church" on Mothering Sunday. "Clypping" means greeting and honouring the church: parishioners troop outside after or during the service, and walk around the church in a big circle holding hands and singing a hymn, then walking in towards the church and outwards again, still holding hands. It is meant as a gesture of love and affection for the parish church. A linked custom is that of visiting the cathedral or "Mother church" of a diocese on this day. On the other hand, some "church clypping" in England is done in September, on the Sunday nearest to Our Lady's Birthday (September 8).

It is a small step, of course, from honouring Mother Church to honouring our natural mothers, and so the custom grew up of boys and girls paying special tribute to their mothers on this day.

"Mothering Sunday" was certainly well established by the 18th and 19th centuries when youngsters working away from home, especially girls "in service" as cooks and maids in other households, would be allowed to go home for the day. They would usually take a basket of goodies with them, and these would include a simnel cake, the name dating back to that special flour used by the ancient Romans.

The custom was given a new boost in the middle of this century, when during World War II a number of American servicemen were stationed in various parts of rural Britain. They brought with them their own tradition of "Mothers' Day", which is a strictly American occasion marked in May. It was started in the 1990s by a Miss Anna Jarvis who thought there ought to be a day in the year when mothers were honoured with gifts of flowers: it became a national crusade and was adopted officially when the United States Congress fixed a day in May as "Mothers' Day". It should not be confused with our Mothering Sunday, which is on a different date in the year. But the Americans, missing their own mothers, transferred their customs— and their gifts of cards and flowers and sweets—to the British families with whom they had become friendly. The popularity of special cards and boxed chocolates for this day dates from this time.

Most of today's Mothering Sunday cards are labelled "Happy Mother's Day".

Some churches—and this seems a nice idea—celebrate Mothering Sunday by distributing small posies of flowers to children in the congregation and having them give them to their mothers. Violets seem the most popular, and a posy of violets is rapidly becoming a symbol of Mothering Sunday. Bunches of daffodils are popular, too.

Mothering Sunday Celebrations

There should be a special lunch and supper on Mothering Sunday—perhaps cooked by the father and children?—and Laetare Sunday is the day when we eat and drink what we like, and relax from any self-imposed penances we have been offering during Lent.

There should be spring flowers on the table—violets, daffodils, whatever you like—and perhaps the mother's place could be specially decorated.

It's worth remembering that the whole Church is celebrating on Mothering Sunday. The Pope may honour someone by giving them a Golden Rose—this is a special spray of flowers, made of gold, blessed by the Pope and sent as a token of affection to some notable person or institution. It is a symbol of spiritual joy. In the heart of the main rose is a tiny cask containing musk and balsam.

The small baskets described under the Easter section as "Easter baskets" could equally well serve for Mothering Sunday gifts, decorated with flowers and filled with sweets or with a pretty posy. Other suitable Mothering Sunday gifts are a hanky, fudge, a scented sachet, or some writing-paper. Gifts should be small and pretty: the "Bumper Mother's Day Gift Pack" type of thing should be avoided. Mothering Sunday is a day when we honour other values than commercial ones.

Simnel Cake

A simnel cake is still the proper gift for a daughter to make for her mother on Mothering Sunday. Now that so many girls leave home to live in flats with friends, it makes sense to revive the old custom of a girl showing off her new cookery skills by turning up at home on Mothering Sunday with a freshly-baked Simnel Cake.

Another nice idea is for a new bride to bake two cakes—one for her mother and one for her mother-in-law on this day.

Simnel cake is eaten on Mothering Sunday as a break from the Lenten fast—and again at Easter, too, if liked. Its special feature is a layer of marzipan baked inside it, and the marzipan eggs on the top—always eleven in number, symbolising the Apostles minus Judas.

You will need:

6 oz. flour
4 oz. butter
4 oz. sugar
6 oz. currants
2 oz. mixed peel
4 oz. muscatel raisins
4 oz. sultanas
2 eggs
1 oz. almonds
1 tablespoon brandy
¼ nutmeg
¼ teaspoon bicarbonate of soda
2 teaspoonfuls vinegar
½ lb. marzipan

Cream the butter and sugar until soft and fluffy, add the eggs, and then the flour, then the fruit and all remaining ingredients (except the marzipan).

Line a large cake-tin with silver foil, both bottom and sides, and *grease it thoroughly*. Put half the mixture in it. Then roll out some marzipan—be generous—and place the cake-tin on top and cut round it to make a circle. Put this circle of marzipan on top of the mixture, and add the other half. Bake in a moderate oven for two and a half to three hours, and then place some grease-proof paper (the paper that was wrapped round the butter will do excellently) over the top and bake for a further half an hour or until a knife inserted into the cake comes out clean.

To decorate: Make another marzipan circle for the top of the cake, and roll out wide strips for the sides. Turn the cake out carefully to cool on a tray while you are preparing all this. When it is cool and ready to decorate, take a good look at it: if it seems very dry or a little over-baked, stand it on a plate and pour generous amounts of sherry over it in a gentle trickle with the aid of a spoon. This dampens the cake—it also makes it taste absolutely delicious!

Remember, too, that if the cake is burnt on top this can be very gently sliced off with a sharp knife. When you come to put the marzipan on the cake, warm the jam and spread this all over the cake with the back of a spoon, being fairly generous. Then place the marzipan on top—the jam will make it stick. Fashion eleven eggs out of the remaining marzipan and put them round the top. Next, you could brown the cake very lightly under the grill, or you can make marzipan lettering spelling out the word "Simnel" or "Mother". Or you could make a criss-cross lattice work out of marzipan, or make some white glacé icing and, using a fine nozzle, write "Simnel" or "Mother" or whatever you like. Tie a wide yellow ribbon round the sides of the cake, or cut a paper frill for it. You could also buy small Easter eggs with which to decorate it, instead of using marzipan ones.

Egg Custard

A Sheffield lady whom I met in a train while working on this book remembered Mothering Sunday from her own childhood in the earlier part of this century: "We always used to have a big egg custard on the Fourth Church Sunday, Mothering Sunday". An egg custard, sweet and creamy, symbolising all the delicious things we normally don't have in Lent, would certainly be a most appropriate dish for the main Mothering Meal:

Make one pound of sweet shortcrust pastry (using butter instead of other fats, and adding one ounce of brown sugar to the flour)
Filling:

> *Three eggs*
> *quarter of a pint of milk and a quarter of a pint of double cream*
> *half a teaspoonful of grated nutmeg*
> *two oz. of brown sugar.*

Line a pretty flan dish with the pastry. Beat the eggs, add the milk and cream, and then the nutmeg and sugar. Pour it into the flan case and bake in a moderate oven until set. Sprinkle a little more nutmeg and sugar on top before serving. You can serve it with cream if you like.

Lancashire Cheese Cake

Mrs M. Cook, of Raynes Park, South London, gave me this lovely recipe of her mother's for cheese cake, after meeting me when I was giving a talk on traditional feasts and seasons at a local Library Circle. I think it might make a very good dish for Mothering Sunday:
One pie dish lined with shortcrust pastry
Filling:

> *2 pints milk (Beastings if possible. Beastings: first milk taken from a cow after calving)*
> *1 tablespoon rennet*
> *1 egg*
> *half an ounce of butter*
> *2 oz. caster sugar*
> *2 oz. currants*

Method:
Warm milk to blood heat. Add rennet. Leave about 10 mins. Turn curd into a fairly fine cloth. Squeeze out all the whey. Run curd through a fine sieve and add to it the beaten egg, the butter (melted) and the sugar. Mix well. Put into the pastry case, sprinkle currants into it and cook at Gas mark 5 for 30 or 40 minutes.

> *I rejoiced at the things that were said to me: We shall go into the house of the Lord.*
> *Our feet were standing in thy courts, O Jerusalem.*
> *Jerusalem, which is built as a city, which is compact together.*
> *For thither did the tribes go up, the tribes of the Lord: the testimony of Israel, to praise the name of the Lord.*
> *Because their seats have sat in judgement, seats upon the house of David.*
> *Pray ye for the things that are for the peace of Jerusalem:*
> *and abundance for them that love thee.*
> *Let peace be in thy strength: and abundance in thy towers.*
> *For the sake of my brethren, and of my neighbours.*
> *I spoke peace of thee.*
> *Because of the house of the Lord our God, I have sought good things for thee.*
>
> *(Ps. 121).*

Springtime Saints

Saints' days make a splash of colour in the gloom of Lent, and there are two important saints for people living in the British Isles during this time—St David and St Patrick. Both are celebrated in some style in their own countries, and they also belong to the worldwide church. At this time of year we also celebrate the feast of one of the best-loved saints of all time, St Joseph.

March 1—St David, patron of Wales

> O great Saint David, still we hear thee call us,
> Unto a life that knows no fear of death;
> Yea, down the ages will thy words enthrall us,
> Strong, happy words: "Be joyful, keep the faith".
> On Cambria's sons stretch out your hands in blessing;
> For our dear land thy help we now implore.
> Lead us to God, with humble hearts confessing
> Jesus, Lord and King for evermore.

St David—or Dewi to give him his Welsh name—was the son of a chieftain in Cardigan. He founded twelve monasteries across Wales, from Croyland to Pembrokeshire. He went on pilgrimage to Jerusalem and there was consecrated a bishop. His life and work made a indelible impression on Wales.

The site of St David's birth—which took place in the 6th century—is said to be Henfynw in Cardigan. His principal monastery was at the place now known as St David's in Pembrokeshire. It was known to be a particularly strict and austere monastery. Its influence spread far and wide, and particularly to Ireland.

There are places of interest linked with St David all across Wales, and you will also find them in South-West England and in Brittany.

The traditional dish to eat on St David's Day is leeks. Many Welsh people will also be wearing daffodils today in his honour.

Traditional Welsh Bread

I learned about bara brith, the traditional Welsh bread with currants, from the wife of a Warrant Officer in the Welsh Guards. "I don't do any measuring, really, I just do it all by sight" she told me in her attractive Welsh lilt. "Seems funny to have the recipe written down—I just got it passed on, you know, from my mother." She's lived in lots of different places around Europe because of her husband's job but she misses Wales: "I miss the singing, and the friendliness, especially in church. In church for St David's Day, with the Guards—you've never heard such beautiful singing."

Bara Brith

> *One pound of self-raising flour*
> *one pound mixed dried fruit*
> *two tablespoons marmalade*
> *one egg*
> *six tablespoons sugar*
> *one cup of cold tea without milk*
> *one teaspoonful of ground mixed spice*

Mix the dried fruit and sugar and soak it overnight in the cold tea.

Next day add the flour, spice and marmalade. Stir and then add the egg.

Line a loaf-tin with greased paper, put the mixture in and cook in a moderate oven for one and a quarter hours. You can glaze the top with honey before putting it in the oven if you like.

You eat the bara brith in thick slices, spread with butter, at tea-time.

St Patrick—March 17: Ireland

> *Hail, glorious St Patrick, dear saint of our isle*
> *On us, thy poor children, bestow a sweet smile*
> *And now thou art high in the mansions above*
> *On Erin's green valleys look down in thy love.*
>
> (*Sister Agnes*)

Irish people won't need reminding about celebrating St Patrick's Day. But others might like to join in, too, and honour this saint whose feast-day will be celebrated all over the world wherever Irish exiles gather. See how many people in your town will be wearing a bit of shamrock today, or a little favour showing a golden harp on a bit of green ribbon.

St Patrick was an ancient Briton, living in the days when Britain was a colony of the Roman Empire and people had adopted many

Roman ways and habits. He was reared in a Christian home: his father was a deacon by the name of Calpurnius. The family lived in what we now call Wales. When he was sixteen he was captured by pirates from across the Irish Sea, and taken back to Ireland where he had to work as a shepherd and swineherd. It was while he was working thus that he had a great spiritual experience and decided that he must serve God in some special way. He eventually returned to his native land and trained as a priest, travelling to Gaul (now France) for some of his studies. After several years, he returned to Ireland as a missionary.

St Patrick's work in Ireland transformed the country and laid the foundations for what it has been ever since. Irish people are rightly proud of their strong Christian heritage, and can point to the thousands of Irish missionaries who have taken the faith to other lands.

St Patrick is said to have converted Ireland's druids by calling down Heavenly fire to show the power of the One True God. He taught people about the mystery of the Trinity by using a shamrock leaf, and made the shamrock the symbol of Ireland that it has been ever since. Legend says that he turned all the snakes off the island, and certainly there are no snakes in Ireland at all to this day. He established his episcopal see at Armagh, where Ireland's Primates still preside.

When Irish emigrants went abroad in the 19th century—driven by the appalling suffering inflicted on them through the potato famine and the heartlessness of absentee (often English) landlords—they took their precious Christian beliefs, their love of the native land, and their devotion to St Patrick with them. St Patrick's Cathedral in New York is the most famous of the landmarks they established in distant lands as proof of their unswerving devotion. On March 17 people in Australia, New Zealand, the USA, England, and every place where people of Irish ancestry gather, will be holding festivities in St Patrick's honour.

You can take a break from Lent in order to celebrate St Patrick's Day if you like. Perhaps the most beautiful prayer that St Patrick left behind—among a number of writings—is his "breastplate". It has been deservedly popular with generations, and it would be a beautiful prayer to read out to the family today.

St Patrick's Breastplate

Christ with me, Christ before me,
Christ behind me, Christ in me,
Christ beneath me, Christ above me,
Christ on my right, Christ on my left,
Christ where I lie, Christ where I sit,
Christ where I arise,
Christ in the heart of every man who thinks of me,
Christ in the mouth of every man who speaks of me,
Christ in every eye that sees me,
Christ in every ear that hears me,
Salvation is of the Lord,
Salvation is of Christ,
May Your Salvation, Lord, be ever with us.

How to Celebrate St Patrick's Day

In Ireland, March 17 is a public holiday. It's also a day when most people attend church. Shamrock is sold on the preceding days, and posted to friends abroad, and greetings cards are sent. The day is generally regarded in Ireland as heralding the coming of spring. Dances and parties are held, many of them out of doors. Everyone wears a sprig of shamrock or a green ribbon favour.

The traditional dish is boiled bacon and cabbage.

Boiled Bacon and Cabbage

To serve four (multiply as needed):

1½ lbs. boiling bacon or ham
cabbage

Wash the bacon and if it is very salty, steep it in cold water for a few hours. Place in a saucepan and cover with cold water. Bring slowly to a boil and simmer, allowing 25 minutes to each pound and 25 minutes extra at the end of cooking. When cooked, remove the bacon, and cook the cabbage in the same water, chopped up. Remove the rind from the bacon. Sprinkle bacon with bread crumbs and place under the grill for a few minutes to brown. Slice the bacon and serve hot with the freshly cooked cabbage. Hot parsley sauce can be served with the bacon, if desired.

St Joseph—March 19

St Joseph was, of course, the spouse and protector of Mary, and foster-father of the Holy Child. He was a carpenter, a hard-working small businessman, a craftsman, a man who bore the heavy responsibility of being the provider and the leader of the family. He is the special guardian of families everywhere, a patron for hard-pressed modern fathers, a man whose role shows the importance and honour which the Christian Church attaches to fatherhood and to family life.

Fathers today may feel worried about their exact role and status. It no longer seems to hold the automatic dignity in the past. The high divorce rate and the social acceptance of illegitimacy seem to have stressed the unimportance and even the irrelevance of a father's role. Into this sadness and confusion the Church sheds light and warmth with the figure of Saint Joseph. We see here a father who had a unique dignity but did not presume on it; a man of honour and integrity; "a just man". It was he whom Our Lord would have had as a model for manhood—he who taught Him the basic skills which earned the family income, he who presided over family worship, discussions, excursions, and festivities.

A Day for Fathers

In Italy, March 19th is a day on which fathers are specially honoured. The traditional food for the day is doughnuts! So try cheering up Dad with doughnuts on St Joseph's day!

Traditional Doughnuts

> *flour (one pound)*
> *yeast (1½ oz)*
> *luke-warm milk (½ pint)*
> *sugar (2 oz)*
> *a pinch of salt*
> *grated peel of one lemon*
> *jam for the filling*
> *cooking oil*
> *and c. (4 oz) sugar for sprinkling on afterwards.*

Mix the ingredients, beating well and letting rise. Then roll out the dough (1 cm thick) on a floured baking tray. Use a wine glass to mark out circles on half of this dough. Put some jam in the middle of each of these circles, brush the edges of the circles with egg-white, and cover with the other half of the dough. Cut out the doughnuts, press the edges together, and let them rise again. Then carefully put the doughnuts (upside down) into the oil (just below boiling). Put a top on the pot for the first 5 minutes so that the doughnuts swell up. Then turn the doughnuts and cook for a further 5 minutes. Put the finished doughnuts on a grid so that the fat can drip off, and sprinkle with sugar while they are still hot.

A Saint for Girls Seeking Husbands

By strong tradition, St Joseph is invoked by girls seeking a good husband. In this, it is nice that his feast comes in the spring which is the time of year we associate with courtship and romance. It is easy to laugh at the idea of praying to St Joseph to find a suitable mate, but I have met too many happily married women who have admitted, "Well, I know it sounds daft, but I'd heard about praying to St Joseph, so I—" to dismiss this good saint's achievements too lightly! Because tradition also says that Joseph was not a young man when he was espoused, he is said to be of help to girls who fear they are getting beyond marriageable age—he likes to confound people! Finally, because he was a carpenter, it is said that he will give you a marvellous husband but also a "knock on the head"—some little, or large, inconvenience attached to your marriage which will just serve to remind you that you can't expect everything to be perfect this side of paradise.

Lady Day—March 25

On March 25 we celebrate the Annunciation—the day on which Mary was told she was to be the mother of the world's Redeemer. Why March 25? Because it is exactly nine months before Christ's birth celebrations on December 25.

Everything in the Church's calendar makes sense. When Mary heard the message of the Angel, she was also told that her cousin Elisabeth was to have a child and was indeed already in her sixth month of pregnancy. So count three months on to complete the pregnancy and you come to June—now turn the pages to that month in this book and read about what we celebrate on Midsummer Day.

The old name for the feast of the Annunciation is Lady Day. In an age which fails to respect unborn life, Lady Day is a day for honouring Christ in the womb of His mother, for celebrating the Incarnation and remembering that when the Word was made flesh, it was as an unborn baby.

Do you know that beautiful prayer, the Angelus? It is said at noon. Some churches still ring out an Angelus bell. You are meant to stop what you are doing for just a couple of minutes, to recall the Incarnation and thank God for it.

V. The angel of the Lord appeared unto Mary.
R. And she conceived of the Holy Spirit.
Hail Mary . . .

V. Behold the handmaid of the Lord.
R. Be it done unto me according to Thy Word.
Hail Mary . . .

V. And the Word was made flesh (bow your head)
R. And dwelt among us.
Hail Mary . . .

V. Pray for us, O Holy Mother of God.
R. That we may be made worthy of the promises of Christ.

Let us pray.
Pour forth, we beseech thee, O Lord, Thy grace into our hearts, that we, to whom the Incarnation of Christ Your Son was made known by the message of an angel, may by His Passion and Death be brought to the glory of the resurrection. Through Christ Our Lord. Amen.

Lady Day used to mark the beginning of the New Year in medieval England. In a sense we still do mark a New Year around this time, because for financial purposes the annual cycle is deemed to go from April 6 to April 6, as our taxation forms remind us.

In recent years there have been moves among Catholics and Anglicans to have a renewed emphasis on the importance of Lady Day. A springtime day honouring the Incarnation, stressing the reverence that we should have for the unborn Christ in His mother's womb would be a useful way of reminding everyone of the basics of our Christian faith.

A part of London commemorates the Annunciation—The Angel, Islington. The district is so called because of a pub of that name. And the pub took its name from its old sign, which showed an Angel giving the news to Mary that she was to be the Mother of the world's Redeemer. Over the years, the pub sign was altered, and just showed an angel. Pubs called "The Salutation" also commemorate the Annunciation and so, oddly enough, do some that are called "The Flower Pot". This is because a flower in a pot was sometimes part of the background to the Annunciation scene in the old medieval paintings. When the Annunciation ceased to appear on the sign, the flower in its pot remained—and was given an undue significance.

Devotion to Mary in the Middle Ages was responsible for forming attitudes towards women in Christian Europe. The idea of chivalry was formed around it: in honouring Mary, men honoured, in a sense, the whole female sex. Women were no longer to be regarded as slaves or playthings for males. They must not be associated with degradation or regarded merely with sensuality. Instead, through Mary, women were to receive a sort of homage, a huge respect. Manners, good taste, and the concept of mutual courtesy were all associated with this. It lingers still in the old ideas about a man taking off his hat to a lady, offering his seat to her in a bus or train, opening a door for her, rising when she enters a room. In denouncing all this, as both males and females (but, alas, especially females) have done in recent years, we have alas denounced a precious part of our heritage.

Lady Day more or less marks the Vernal Equinox—the day in spring when day and night are of the same length. So it lies immediately between the winter solstice (more or less at Christmas) which is the shortest day, and the summer solstice in June which is the longest day.

Explaining Britain's Calendar

It was the timing of Lady Day that brought about a major calendar change, which affected all of Britain's dates and is worth explaining.

The modern calendar that we use is called the Gregorian Calendar, because it was first introduced during the reign of Pope Gregory XIII in 1582. That year, the international authorities, brought together in Rome, reported on a serious anomaly that had emerged with regard to the way in which the date was calculated. Everyone had been using the Julian Calendar, introduced a long while before. Lady Day, March 25th, was always supposed to coincide with the Vernal Equinox. But in 1582 the equinox, which had certainly fallen on

March 25th in the time of Julius Caesar, actually fell on March 11th. This was because the old Julian calculation of 365 and a quarter days per year was in fact 11 minutes and ten seconds too much. The extra days had built up and caused an error.

It was decided to sort the matter out, suppress ten days so as to make the equinox fall on March 21st, and then carry on under an adjusted system. This was done, with Pope Gregory lending his authority, and his name, to the move. But Britain did not in fact adopt his new calendar until nearly two hundred years later, in 1752. It was then introduced in September of that year, when eleven days had to be suppressed to get the dates into order: Wednesday September 2nd was followed by Thursday September 14th.

There were riots, arguments, and disagreements, as thousands of ordinary people felt confused and cheated. "Give us back our eleven days!" was the cry, and resentment lingered on for years. People felt that things would never be the same again, and indeed since that time there certainly have been some confusions. Hawthorn blossom, for instance, was long ago given the name May because it used to bloom in that month. Now the blossoms appear in June. The Glastonbury Thorn (see section under Christmas) is sometimes said to bloom on old Christmas Day, January 6th, rather than the new one of December 25th.

Our tax and financial year focuses around April 6th, Old Lady Day.

And just to confuse things, a society was formed in Oxford earlier this century with the aim of restoring the missing eleven days!

Holy Week

We adore Thee, O Christ, and we praise Thee
Because by Thy Holy Cross Thou hast redeemed the world.

Easter is approaching. Why do we celebrate Easter each year on the date that we do? Christina Hole in *Easter and its Customs* tells us that the custom dates back to the days of the very earliest Christians: "In those first years it was not kept every year on the same day. Because Christ died and rose again during the Passover period, many observed Easter on that festival, keeping the Passover as their ancestors had done before them, but seeing it now illuminated by a new and different Light. Others, especially the Gentiles of the Western communities, kept it on the Sunday following, remembering that it was on the morning after the Sabbath "the first day of the week" that Mary Magdalen saw her risen Lord in the dawnlit garden and thought He was the gardener. This difference of custom continued for a long time, and eventually resulted in serious controversies between the Churches of East and West. "In AD 325, the Council of Nicaea ruled that the festival should be celebrated, not on the Passover which might fall on any day of the week but on the Sunday following the first full moon after (or on) the Vernal Equinox, that Equinox being deemed to occur always on March 21: and that if the moon happened to be full on a Sunday, then Easter day should be on the Sunday after. Thus it is that throughout Western Christendom still, the great religious feast of spiritual hope is governed in its date by the Spring moon, and can never be earlier than March 22 or later than April 25."

We often describe Easter as the Paschal season. This comes from the Hebrew word *pesach*, meaning Passover. The French word for Easter echoes it, as does the Italian.

Palm Sunday

They took branches of palm and went out to meet
Him, shouting "Hosanna! Blessings on the King of
Israel, who comes in the name of the Lord"
(John. 12:12–16)

Palm Sunday marks the beginning of Holy Week. We walk into church in procession bearing palm branches and remembering

Christ's entry into Jerusalem, an account of His subsequent Passion is read aloud. We are reaching the climax of the Church's year, the commemoration of what Jesus Christ did for us.

Some palms are distributed made into the shape of crosses, others are just long natural wands (which I happen to prefer—it seems a stronger link with the Gospel story). Palms should never be discarded once they are brought home, but treated with respect as they have been used in a sacred ceremony. Many families put them somewhere on display, tucked up behind a statue or a crucifix in a bedroom or in the kitchen. A small palm in the shape of a cross can be kept in a prayer-book.

Last year's leftover palms in church were burned to make the ashes for this year's Ash Wednesday ceremonies. If you like, you can burn your own old palm on Ash Wednesday and watch it turn after a brief flare into soft ashes (hold it over the sink and light the end with a match. It will burn quickly, and you have water on hand in case of problems).

Palms could be put on the table for Sunday lunch on Palm Sunday, and branches of pussy-willow—which is often called palm—make a nice decoration, too. The meal could include some sort of a pie, with a cross on top of the pastry to mark the start of Holy Week: a Palm Sunday Pie.

Spy Wednesday

The Wednesday of Holy Week is known as Spy Wednesday to commemorate the activities of the traitor Judas.

Maundy Thursday—Holy Thursday

> *I give you a new commandment:*
> *love one another as I have loved you.*

The word "Maundy" comes from the Latin *Mandatum* meaning an order or command. It refers to Christ's final command to us via His Apostles, given at the Last Supper: that we must love one another as he loves us. To show this love. He got down on His knees before the meal and washed the Apostles' feet one by one. On Maundy Thursday during what we call the Mandatum, the priest will wash the feet of twelve parishioners. This ceremony will be performed in Rome, where the Pope will wash the feet of twelve elderly Romans. In London's Westminster Cathedral the Cardinal will wash the feet of twelve Chelsea Pensioners. And in parishes around the globe, parish priests will be kneeling and washing the feet of altar-servers with the same gesture.

Maundy Money

Our Sovereign, too, commemorates Our Lord's actions—though not in full style. The present Queen does not wash anyone's feet—the last monarch to do that was our last Catholic King, James II. An old document describes the scene saying that he "on Maundy Thursday April 16th 1685 . . . wash'd, wiped and kiss'd the feet of 52 poor men with wonderful humility." The figure of 52 corresponded to his age. The old custom is still remembered with the distribution of Maundy money to elderly men and women in a special service held in one of our country's ancient cathedrals and attended by the Queen and Prince Philip. The Queen gives out the money—specially minted coins in special purses—to as many men and women as there are years in her age. It is a colourful ceremony with a number of interesting touches, including the distribution of posies of flowers to all the principal participants. This is not, as is often widely stated, a relic of the old days when it was thought that the flowers would ward off any infection from the elderly and sick people, but because they would ward off any nasty *smell*—which I daresay they most effectively did! The Maundy Money replaces gifts of cloth and food given in former times.

It might be nice for children to receive Maundy money—one coin of each denomination, polished up and put in a decorative envelope with the child's name on it, waiting by the child's plate at the supper table. Money looks quite different when it has been cleaned and polished up, and feels very special.

The Holy Thursday Mass

In Catholic churches, the Holy Thursday Mass is the Mass of the Last Supper and so is held in the evening. During the Gloria, all the bells in the church are rung. They will not be heard again until Holy Week is over, and everyone can be joyful once more on Easter Sunday.

Holy Thursday honours the day that Our Lord ate His Last Supper with His Apostles: the day He took bread and wine and celebrated the first Mass—that action that has since been repeated so many millions of times down the centuries and across the globe.

During the Consecration on Maundy Thursday, the priest will say "On the night before He suffered—that is TONIGHT" and all present will realise that they are commemorating events that changed the course of history.

At the end of Mass, the Blessed Sacrament will be taken away to an Altar of Repose where everyone can take a turn at watching and praying with Our Lord. The main altar will be stripped bare, the candles put out and taken away, the altarcloths removed, the sanctuary lamp left unlit, the tabernacle door swinging open. It is a scene of desolation, and will remain that way until the splendour of the Easter liturgy, when it will be a riot of flowers and candles.

The Altar of Repose will usually be a side altar, always decorated with flowers and turned into a garden scene. People remember Gethsemane. Most parishes draw up a rota to ensure that there is always someone watching with Our Lord until midnight. There is something rather wonderful about hurrying out from home in the dark to share some time with Him, joining other shadowy figures in this candlelit garden-corner of the darkened church.

> *"Love is His word, Love is His way*
> *Feasting with men, fasting alone*
> *Living and dying, rising again,*
> *Love, only love, is His way.*
> *Richer than gold is the love of my Lord;*
> *Better than splendour and wealth.*
>
> *Love is His way, love is His mark,*
> *Sharing His last Passover feast,*
> *Christ at the table, host to the Twelve,*
> *Love, only love, is His mark.*
>
> *Love is His mark, love is His sign*
> *Bread for our strength, wine for our joy*
> *'This is my body, this is my Blood'*
> *Love, only love, is His sign.*
>
> *Love is His sign, love is His news,*
> *'Do this' He said 'Lest you forget*
> *All my deep sorrow, all my dear blood'*
> *Love, only love, is His news.*
>
> *Love his His news, Love is His name*
> *We are His own, chosen and called,*
> *Family brethren, cousins and kin,*
> *Love, only love, is His name.*

Love is His name, love is His law.
Hear His command, all who are His:
'Love one another, I have loved you.'
Love, only love, is His law.

Love is His law, love is His word:
Love of the Lord, Father and Word,
Love of the Spirit, God ever one
Love, only love, is His word."

(Luke Connaughton)

The Passover Meal

Meanwhile, how can we mark Holy Thursday in our homes? This is the Passover Night, the night when Christ, after the Passover Meal, was to shed His Blood for us. The traditional thing to eat is roast lamb cooked with herbs, the same basic food as the Jews ate and still eat at their Passover. We should feel an affinity with the Jewish people tonight, and remember them in our prayers. We can also feel an affinity with our own ancestors, who at this Springtime season, after the lack of fresh meat throughout the winter, and then the harsh fasting of Lent, would enjoy fresh roast lamb and see the symbolism of the world made new and the Good News of Christ in this Paschal season, as we should.

'The Lord said to Moses and Aaron in the land of Egypt, 'This month is to be the first of all the others for you, the first month of your year, speak to the whole community of Israel and say, On the tenth day of this month each man must take an animal from the flock, one for each family: one animal for each household. If the household is too small to eat the animal, a man must join with his neighbour, the nearest to his house, as the number of persons requires. You must take into account what each can eat in deciding the number for the animal. It must be an animal without blemish, a male one year old; you may take it from either sheep or goats. You must keep it till the fourteenth day of the month when the whole assembly of the community of Israel shall slaughter it between two evenings. Some of the blood must then be taken and put on the two doorposts and the lintel of the houses where it is eaten. That night, the flesh is to be eaten, roasted over the fire; it must be eaten with unleavened bread and bitter herbs. You shall eat it like this: with a girdle round your waist, sandals on your feet, a staff in your hand:

106

You shall eat it hastily: it is a passover in honour of the Lord. That night, I will go through the land of Egypt and strike down all the first-born in the land of Egypt, man and beast alike, and I shall deal out punishment to all the gods of Egypt, I am the Lord. The blood shall serve to mark the houses that you live in. When I see the blood I will pass over you and you shall escape the destroying plague when I strike the land of Egypt. This day is to be a day of remembrance for you, and you must celebrate it as a feast in the Lord's honour. For all generations you are to declare it a day of festival, forever.'

(Exodus 12: 1—8, 11—14)

If the whole family is to attend the Holy Thursday Mass, the roast lamb could be prepared at home and left cooking in a very low oven ready to dish up on everyone's return. If people are hurring out at some stage to take their turn at the Altar of Repose, the Old Testament reading about eating the meal in a hurry and ready for a journey will seem very appropriate!

If it is not convenient to eat the roast lamb tonight, it could be eaten after the Easter vigil, on Saturday night. It makes a delicious late supper, again cooked in a slow oven while everyone is at church. One advantage of eating it then is that there is a greater sense of the Passover having been completed—Christ is risen and we can now feast with complete enjoyment, and our Easter candles lend a glow to the scene. Alternatively, it could be eaten for Easter Sunday lunch, and once again it welcomes us with its delicious fragrance as we enter the house hungry for the meal.

Roast Lamb with Garlic

You can choose whatever joint you like that is suitable for the number of people you will be having for the meal. Stand the joint on its roasting-dish, and with a very sharp knife make deep slits at regular intervals all over it. Into each slit press a clove, or a piece of a clove, of garlic. Make sure you press the garlic right down into the meat: the slits will really need to be quite deep. Sprinkle salt, and some rosemary, generously over the top, and cover the joint with silver foil. Give it long, slow cooking at the bottom of the oven. Rosemary has long been regarded as a very special herb: old country lore says that a rosemary plant grows for 33 years—the lifetime of Our Lord.

You should make some herbal stuffing to serve alongside the lamb: a lot of it. Sage and onion is very good, together with onion sauce in a separate dish.

Do not serve potatoes with the meal: it must be bread to be traditional. The best bread to use is pita bread, which is obtainable in most supermarkets.

In Germany Maundy Thursday is known as Grun Donnerstag— Green Thursday. This may be because of the herbs that are eaten with the roast lamb on this day.

"There's rosemary, that's for remembrance".

All in the April evening, April airs were abroad
The sheep with their little lambs passed me by on the road;
The sheep with their little lambs passed me by on the road—
All in the April evening, I thought of the Lamb of God.
The lambs were weary and crying, with a weak human cry:
I thought of the lamb of God, going meekly to die ...

Up in the blue, blue mountains, dewy pastures are sweet:
Rest for the little bodies, rest for the little feet.
But for the Lamb, the Lamb of God
Up on the hilltop green:
Only a Cross, a Cross of shame
Two stark crosses between.

All in the April evening, April airs were abroad:
I saw the sheep with their lambs, and thought of the Lamb of God.

Holy Week Ideas

Holy Week should be a time when there is plenty to do and to think about:

- If there is a Passion Play, or a performance of a musical work such as Bach's St Matthew Passion in your area during Holy Week, why not go along? It will be money well spent. I remember a superb St Matthew Passion one Maundy Thursday in Berlin, sung by the St Hedwig Cathedral Choir in the Philharmonie a few yards from the Berlin Wall: never had the sin and folly of man, bearing down on the Man in the Garden, seemed so intense. I remember another superb Passion sung at London's Royal Festival Hall which I attended with a group of friends, going back for a buffet meal (this was Palm Sunday) laid out at the flat of one of them. For adults, hearing the tale of Christ's Passion told really well in drama or in music can bring its message home with all the sharp intensity with which we heard it as children.

● It is a good idea to borrow from the local record library, or even to buy, some suitable music to have around the house at Easter. The Passion as just described, some settings of the Mass—and why not the Hallelujah Chorus for Easter Sunday? Try a browse through the "sacred music" section in the record library and use this opportunity to widen the family's tastes beyond pop, punk, and advertising jingles.

● Easter cards have not become an excuse for a big commercial spree as have Christmas cards. It is possible simply to send them to friends or family without pressure. Why not make your own—with pressed flowers if it's an early spring? Send the children out to see what they can find—or use pressed flowers from last summer (see under "May" for instructions on pressing flowers). Simply mount the flowers on to stiff paper or cardboard with tiny dabs of glue. Quotations from the Exulstet make beautiful wording for the lettering to go underneath, instead of the banal "Happy Easter" which somehow fails to convey real joy. Use "Letraset" or get a book from the library on how to do elaborate lettering.

● Ideas for Easter decorations, gifts, etc., will be found under the Easter section. It is much more fun, and more interesting, to make your own Easter trimmings than merely to buy lots of boxed gimmicky Easter eggs, and the work gives a sense of Easter-is-getting-nearer growing excitement to younger members of the family.

● The Stations of the Cross are a particularly suitable devotion for Holy Week. All Catholic churches, and some Anglican ones, have these fourteen poignant memorials of Christ's walk to Calvary along their walls. Children like to "do the stations"—it gives them a feeling of ritual and of "specialness" for Holy Week. At its simplest, making the Stations of the cross simply involves walking slowly round a church and meditating and saying a short prayer before each one. There are, of course, also special Stations of the Cross services for the whole parish, which adults will want to attend.

● It sounds morbid, but children sometimes like to act out Passiontide themes for themselves. The Passion play is a very old Christian art form and can be done with tremendous dignity. We can help young actors by looking up possible play scripts for them to use if they are really interested (the library again will be your ally here—try the "Plays" section and see if they have any religious plays that are labelled for schools).

● Old people's homes usually get various treats at Christmas—but what about *Easter*? Wouldn't it be possible to get together with a couple of other local families, and fill a pretty basket with some Easter eggs, sign a home-made card and take it along with a blessed palm to some people who'd appreciate the gesture? (The parish priest will almost certainly have several spare palms—all you have to do is ask for them).

Good Friday

> *Hot Cross Buns!*
> *Hot Cross Buns!*
> *If you have no daughters, give them your sons!*
> *One a penny, two a penny,*
> *Hot Cross Buns!*

Good Friday should start with toasted Hot Cross Buns for breakfast. They are delicious fresh from the grill or toaster with plenty of butter and with cups of tea or coffee. From the beginning, today feels and tastes different from any other day in the year.

Alas, for so many people in modern Britain, Good Friday is simply like a Bank Holiday. Shops—and especially discount stores and drive-in cash-and-carry establishments—are open, the television runs special holiday sporting features. Every year, it seems to get just a little bit more secularised. In some areas of our big cities, you would hardly know that this was a day of any historical, much less spiritual, significance at all.

But it is perfectly possible with just a small amount of thought to make Good Friday into a really special and memorable day that has a quality of its own.

It's worth finding out about some Good Friday traditions. Perhaps there are some in your local area?

The old Anglo-Saxon name for Good Friday was "Langfredag" or "Long Friday", the word "long" being used in the sense of "great". In parts of Sussex it used to be known as "Long Rope Day" and in Brighton there used to be a tradition of everyone taking ropes and skipping with them on the beach on this day. Was this because of the tradition that our Lord was bound with ropes on this day as He was led out to die? Although skipping seems a flippant way of commemorating this, it does emphasise that His death, although terrible, was in a sense a joyful event since it won us our salvation. Skipping on the seashore was also a tradition at Scarborough in the North of England, with fishermen turning the ropes for the children on this day. An old country custom in Britain, observed widely for many years, was that blacksmiths would not hammer in nails to shoe horses on Good Friday, because of the actions of those who nails Christ to the Cross. Similarly, people did not do household jobs that used nails. Wine was also not drunk, because Christ remained thirsty on the Cross.

Planting Seeds

Good Friday is the traditional day for planting seeds—an echo here of the idea of Our Lord's dying and being buried to rise again, of His Blood spilling into the soil and making it fertile.

A Yorkshire lady told me that potatoes were always planted on Good Friday in her childhood, but that no one went out into the garden until twelve o'oclock. (was this because of the tradition that Christ began the final hours of this passion at twelve?)

It is a nice idea for families to plant some seeds today: if you haven't a garden, fill a window-box or some pots. Children love the excitement of seeing the first tiny shoots come up as the days go by, and the wonder of it all is part of the essence of spring. Marigolds are particularly easy: they will grow almost anywhere. Or try mustard-and-cress which has the added pleasure of being able to be eaten in salads or sandwiches for tea!

Planting seeds on Good Friday also commemorates Christ's words about the grain of wheat that must fall into the ground and die, and how they applied to Himself.

Good Friday Activities

O come and mourn with me awhile
See, Mary calls us to her side;
O, come and let us mourn with her
Jesus, our love, Jesus our love, is crucified.

Good Friday should be a special day, a family day, a quiet day, and most emphatically not really a television day. Instead, there are preparations to make for Easter, the meatless Good Friday lunch to prepare, and special Good Friday activities such as decorating the Lenten charts (see earlier) and making an Easter garden.

Many areas hold special inter-church services on Good Friday, usually around midday. Sometimes these include a "Walk of Witness" through the town and the erection of a plain wooden cross on some public site. It is good for Christians of different denominations to join together in this way and taking part in an open-air service to this type can be a memorable and moving experience.

The special Good Friday afternoon service, with its three parts; the reading of the Passion, the Veneration of the Cross, and Holy Communion should for adults be the focal point of Good Friday, and most parishes also have the Stations of the Cross in the evening.

If you have older children, it might be an idea to drive out somewhere special to take part in the Good Friday services: is there a convent or shrine near you which has open-air Stations of the Cross? or a church with a particular musical tradition which would make the Good Friday services memorable?

For younger children—and for grown-ups, too, when they aren't at church—part of the day can be spent creating an Easter garden that will be a focal point for the Easter morning breakfast table.

Making an Easter Garden

First you will need to go out for a walk to collect the necessary bits and pieces. Everyone should carry a suitable box or bag—polythene bags will be useful for the moss and soil—in which to bring home the various things.

Collect:

moss (you will find it growing around the roots of trees)
attractive stones and pebbles

shells if you live near the sea
some nice damp earth
small strong pieces of twig suitable for making miniature fences and
crosses
flowers—daisies and celandines.
You will also want:
some carrot tops
a small handbag mirror
a large plastic or tin tray or plate, or the lid of an old tin box.

You make the garden by putting a layer of soil on the tray and
planting the moss on it. Create a little "lake" by putting the mirror
in a suitable corner and carefully planting moss and pebbles round
it. Carrot tops, if stood on wet moss and watered every day, will start
to sprout and look like miniature ferns. (You can start them off in
a saucer a few days before if you like). In one corner of the tray,
create a hill or mound using earth and pebbles—you could use a
small box or upturned cup with which to start if off. This will be
your Calvary. Cover it with moss and on the top stand three
crosses—one larger than the other two and placed in the centre—
which you have made of the wood you have collected. The horizontal
bar of the cross can be attached to the upright one with "square
lashing". It looks nice to use purple embroidery silk. An alternative
idea is to use three of the family's palms from Palm Sunday, if they
are the sort that have been made up into crosses—but you will
probably find it hard to make them stand upright.

Almost anything can be used to make the garden look pretty.
Shells, stones, and a miniature fence round the edge, a cobbled path
leading up to the Hill of Crosses and made of tiny pebbles.

You will find that if you keep the moss and earth very damp, small
flowers—early daisies and celandines—will keep alive for a few days
if tucked into it. One idea is to leave the garden free of flowers until
the evening of Holy Saturday and then it can be transformed into a
bower for Easter, with white and gold ribbons decorating the
crosses, and flowers everywhere.

If you don't like the artificial look of using a mirror to create a
lake, you could try making a real lake by sinking a small saucer into
the earth with some pebbles in it.

People who are very artistic and clever are even able to fashion ways
of creating an empty tomb, with a stone ready to roll away from the
door on Easter morning, when the tomb is strewn with flowers.

On Good Friday evening, the older members of the family can put the Garden on the table, and turn out the lights and have candles on either side of it, and pray together.

Catholics pray "The Sorrowful Mysteries of the Rosary" on this day:

1. The Agony in the Garden.
"Then Jesus came with them into a country place which is called Gethsemane; and He said to His disciples: Sit you here, while I go yonder and pray ... And going a little further, he fell upon His face, praying, and saying: My Father, if it be possible, let this chalice pass from me. Nevertheless, not as I will, but as Thou wilt."

> Say slowly:
> Our Father ... (once)
> Hail Mary ... (ten times)
> Glory be to the Father, and to the Son, and to the Holy Sprit, as it was in the beginning, is now, and ever shall be, world without end. Amen.
> O my Jesus, forgive us our sins. Save us from the fires of Hell.
> Bring all souls to Heaven, especially those most in need of Thy mercy.

2. The Scouring.
"And Pilate, seeing that he prevailed nothing, but that rather a tumult was made; taking water washed his hands before the people saying; I am innocent of the blood of this just man ... and having scourged Jesus, delivered Him unto them to be crucified."

> Our Father ...
> Hail Mary ...
> Glory be to the Father ...
> O my Jesus, forgive us our sins ...

3. The Crowning with Thorns.
"And stripping him, they put a scarlet cloak about him. And plaiting a crown of thorns, they put it upon his head."

> Our Father ...
> Hail Mary ...
> Glory be to the Father ...
> O my Jesus, forgive us our sins ...

4. The Carrying of the Cross.
"And after they had mocked Him, they took off the cloak from Him, and put on Him His own garments, and led Him away to crucify Him."

114

Our Father ...
Hail Mary ...
Glory be to the Father ...
O my Jesus, forgive us our sins ...

5. The Crucifixion
   "And Jesus, again crying with a loud voice, yielded up His spirit."

Our Father ...
Hail Mary ...
Glory be to the Father ...
O my Jesus, forgive us our sins ...

Good Friday should be a memorable day, with a feeling of silence about it, a meditative quality.

Good Friday in Folklore and Tradition

In the course of compiling this book, I came across many different Good Friday memories and traditions from different places. A lady from Newcastle remembered that in the 1930s children from the different Sunday schools went to a big rally in the main square for an open-air service: "We were each given an orange—these were eaten with great relish and somehow tasted quite different from ordinary oranges. Also, this was the day on which we all wore our new Spring clothes for the first time."

In some homes, Good Friday was time for spring cleaning. In others, seeds were planted and the garden tidied in the morning, but no one could go into the garden after twelve o'clock. Some people maintained that this was the best day in the year for planting potatoes.

In some parts of Germany, spiky branches are brought into the house—a reminder of the Crown of Thorns that Christ wore. The branches are put in water to bloom on Easter Day.

Some people consider that rain on Good Friday is a good sign—a blessing for the year ahead.

> *On the Cross lifted*
> *Thy face I scan*
> *Bearing that Cross for me*
> *Son of Man.*
> *Thorns from Thy diadem*
> *Rough wood Thy throne*

For us Thy cross is borne
Us alone.

No pillow under Thee
To rest Thy head
Only the wooden Cross
Is Thy bed
I read Thy title, Lord
Inscribed above
"Jesus of Nazareth"
King of Love.

Easter Eggs and Gifts

Battle is O'er, hell's armies flee
Raise we the cry of Victory!
Our abounding joy resounding
Alleluia! Alleluia!

There are all sorts of lovely things to make for Easter, and the last
few days of Lent and Holy Week can be spent making them.

Easter Baskets

Children might like to make Easter baskets to hold the eggs which
they are giving to their parents or to other relations, or they might
find these baskets useful themselves for an Easter-egg hunt.
To make a basket you will need:

> An empty washing-up liquid bottle
> some metal polish
> one and a half yards of yellow ribbon, a quarter of an inch wide
> some cotton and a needle
> a pair of sharp scissors
> a ruler

Start by cleaning all the print off the washing-up liquid bottle with
the metal polish—you will find that it comes off fairly easily on to
a piece of wadding or an old rag if you rub hard.

Then cut off the bottle about four inches from the bottom. This
bottom piece will be your basket. Around the top of it put dots about
a quarter of an inch apart. Using a ruler, draw a line from each of
these down to the base. Now cut carefully down each line, and

spread out the basket so that it looks like a star. Then take your ribbon and, starting at the bottom, weave it in and out between these fronds, pulling the basket into shape as you do so. Glue or staple the ends of the ribbon in place. Make the basket's handle by cutting a piece from the remains of the washing-up-liquid bottle and wrapping a ribbon round it or painting designs on it if you like. Fasten it to the basket by making a tiny hole at the end of the handle and on one of the uprights of the basket and sewing it on using a needle and thread. Do the same at the handle's other end. Or you can staple it on if you like.

The basket can now be filled with tissue paper or some straw, and is ready for using for miniature eggs, chocolate bunnies, small gifts, or whatever you want. You could decorate it some more by adding artificial flowers to it: twisting them round the handle or stitching them carefully to the ribbon. Another idea is to put a yoghurt carton inside and fill it with water and use the basket as a vase with a posy of fresh violets in it.

An Easter Branch

An Easter branch is a very decorative thing to have on your sideboard during Easter, and is fun to make.

On Holy Saturday, pick or buy some tree wands or twigs that are just beginning to bud or leaf. Almost anything will do that seems to be sprouting: the one thing to avoid is evergreen which is associated with Christmas. The emphasis here must be on the pale new leaves of spring. You want nice long branches, and they look particularly attractive in a jug with tall daffodils and branches of pussy-willow.

Decorations

On your Easter branch, you will hang various decorations and directions for these are given below.

The most obvious Easter decorations are eggs—symbolic of new life and having inside them the white and gold colours of Easter. To use eggs as decorations, you want only the shells. To achieve a whole egg-shell ready for decoration, you must blow the egg. You do this by making a tiny hole at either end of the egg (you can buy, in most hardware shops, a device for doing this: a sort of plastic holder with a tiny spike in it) and then blow gently but firmly through the egg. The contents will eventually come out through the hole at the other end. Personally, I find this a rather laborious and messy process, and I rather dislike the idea of using the blown contents afterwards (although, if you're less fastidious, they are of course perfectly all right for cooking) but it is not actually difficult to acquire the knack and it is the traditional way of making Easter-egg decorations and people have been doing it for generations. The egg-shell can now be decorated in any way you like.

The prettiest eggs, in my opinion, are those decorated by having material stuck on them: small shapes cut out offelt, or panels of different materials carefully pieced together to cover the whole egg, the joins covered by strips of pretty braid.

Eggs can also be painted with the paints sold for painting boys' plastic construction kits. Suitable Easter symbols might be little flowers, the Alpha and Omega signs, a Cross, the ChiRho symbol, Easter chicks, baby lambs, a church with a steeple. For best results, give the egg a coat of clear varnish before painting. You can also cut out pictures from last year's Easter cards or old birthday cards to stick on the eggs.

Easter Egg Decorations

If you don't want to blow eggs, you can use ordinary broken egg-shells as decorations. Save all the shells of eggs used in cooking the weeks before, and wash them carefully. A broken shell with a small baby chick inside (you can buy tiny fluffy chicks in the shops for a few pence each) looks very engaging. Other broken shells can be decorated in just the same way as whole ones, with the addition of something on the inside, too. It is fun to make very tiny mobiles—perhaps a heart or a flower—and hang them from cotton on the inside of the egg. Use very strong glue to hold the cotton in place.

Other decorations could include small cardboard ChiRho signs to hang from your Easter branch, fluffy chicks made from two yellow woollen balls, a small one for the head and a larger one for the body, with felt eyes and a felt beak stuck on, and cardboard cut-out Easter bunnies made by drawing round a bunny-shaped pastry-cutter.

Small edible items can also go on your Easter branch but they must not be too heavy. Small hollow chocolate eggs are all right, but some solid ones may make it topple over.

118

All items hanging on your Easter branch will need cotton on them: use pretty embroidery silk in yellow or green. You will need very strong glue and some patience to stick it to the blown eggs.

Your palms, if you have not used them for the Easter Garden, might look nice stuck in the vase alongside the other branches.

Broken egg-shells can also be used as tiny vases for Easter: wash them and decorate them, put them in egg-cups, and fill them with water and arrange tiny posies in them.

A basket full of blown and decorated eggs with flowers and wisps of straw tucked around them makes a pretty centrepiece for an Easter breakfast table.

On Holy Saturday there is an air of excitement and anticipation. There are no services in church: a great silence has descended. We are all waiting for tomorrow.

> *And they departing, made the sepulchre sure,*
> *sealing the stone, and setting guards.*
>
> *Matthew 27:66.*

Easter Sunday

> *Let the angelic choirs rejoice!*
> *Let the divine mystery rejoice!*
> *Let the trumpet of salvation resound for so great a King!*
> *Let the earth also rejoice; illumined with splendour, and,*
> *enlightened by the brightness of the eternal King, let it feel that the*
> *darkness of the whole world is dispersed!*
>
> (from the *Exultet*)

The Easter Vigil

Undoubtedly one of the most exciting ways to celebrate Easter is to take part in the Easter vigil ceremony. Here, on the night of Christ's Resurrection, we hear the story of our Redemption from the beginning, and hail Him as the "Alpha and Omega, the beginning and the end", and see His Light shining out to all the world.

Gathering in the dusk in the church porch, watching the Paschal Candle being lit from the Easter fire, is very exciting when you are a child and clutching your own candle tightly, and it takes a fairly hardened adult to be unmoved by it, too. Many churches use special candles for Easter, embossed with the Alpha and Omega symbols. They are taken home afterwards, and can be used on the Easter breakfast and lunch tables.

If candle wax is spilt on coats and on prayer-books, remember that this can be remedied by the use of an iron and blotting-paper. One way to avoid wax spilling is to make a cone of stiff paper and push the base of your candle through it so that all drips are caught.

Easter Morning

Why not an "Easter bonnet"—a new hat for Easter? Having something new for Spring, worn for the first time to church on Easter morning, will help to celebrate the specialness of the season. I am cross that we ordinary folk are not allowed to wear hats much these days. You rarely get the chance to wear one except to weddings, unless you are the Princess of Wales. Who will join me in re-starting a tradition of wearing pretty hats for special occasions—counting Easter as a special occasion?

Easter Morning Breakfast

Every family has its own Easter traditions. Some children are sent out to hunt for eggs that have been hidden all over the house and garden by an Easter hare. In other families, everyone is given and receives Easter eggs like Christmas presents. Whatever happens, Easter is a time for being generous in the matter of eggs and chocolate—there should be a feeling of feast and superabundance!

Easter seems a good time for giving religious gifts: a prayer-book, a medal or a cross and chain. You can buy very attractive decorated eggs, wooden, cardboard or plastic, specially designed for holding Easter gifts. It is fun to fill these with a variety of different things: perhaps lots of small eggs, a chocolate bunny, a fluffy chick, and a Rosary or a holy card. Look out for good quality religious items when on holiday: sometimes the souvenir shops at England's famous churches or cathedrals sell attractive items and it is worth spending a bit more so as to acquire something that is really pleasing to the eye instead of a tawdry plastic statue or holy water stoop!

Easter Breakfast Eggs

The right thing to eat for Easter morning breakfast is of course boiled eggs. These can be decorated in lots of ways. You can add various colourings to the water: onion skins turn eggshells a deep yellow, beetroot juice a lovely pink, nettle leaves a good green, vinegar added to the water makes all the colours brighter. Rubbing with salad oil produces a shine to finish off. You can buy small pellets of egg colouring if you ask around in the shops at Easter. Similarly, some shops sell egg transfers. Or you can paint the eggs as you have done the blown ones.

Another idea is to draw or paint faces on the eggs—but make sure that you use something that will not come off while they are cooking. Felt-tip pens are no good, but a ball-point pen, though fiddly to use, can produce good results. One year, we all got caricatures of famous people—it was fun, and not unsatisfying, to be knocking a Cabinet member on the head at breakfast! Children's wax crayons can be useful for drawing on eggs: they provide a variety of colours, and the wax will melt away leaving the colouring behind.

It is nice to have special hot rolls to eat with the eggs on Easter Sunday morning.

It seems a pity to throw away prettily decorated shells of boiled breakfast eggs—washed carefully they could be extra decorations on your Easter branch, or tiny flower vases for the Easter lunch table.

Pace Egg Rolling

My Lancastrian sister-in-law introduced Pace egg rolling into our family. In Preston, families roll their Easter eggs down the hillside at Avenham Park, which leads down to the valley and the river Ribble.

Egg-rolling has now crossed the Atlantic and annually hundreds of small Americans now assemble on the lawns of the White House in Washington to roll their eggs.

No one seems to know how the idea originated. It is certainly very old—probably pre-Christian and perhaps part of some ancient fertility rite to placate the gods and goddesses of spring. But some people say it symbolises the rolling away of the stone at the entrance to Our Lord's tomb. The word "pace" means paschal.

In any case, it is fun to roll eggs. Originally, of course, hard-boiled eggs were used. But you can use chocolate eggs if you like. Don't unwrap them! Go up to a local hillside, and start rolling them down. Only when an egg cracks against something and is broken can you eat it. You'd be surprised how hardy an Easter egg in its foil wrapping can be, and how much you want it to break when you see other people already munching theirs! If you haven't got a handy hillside, you can roll eggs to each other in a garden or even—with often hilarious results—across a living-room floor.

Easter Lunch

The traditional dish for an Easter lunch is roast lamb (see under Maundy Thursday for a recipe or try the ones below). If you've already eaten lamb on Thursday, you could follow the current fashion and buy a turkey. It now seems very popular to have a turkey at Easter as well as at Christmas. To make it different from the Christmas meal, you could serve it with new potatoes and butter, and a variety of salads, instead of with roast potatoes and boiled vegetables. Another traditional Easter dish is veal.

Some people serve a Christmas pudding afterwards, having made two on "Stir Up Sunday" and eaten one on Christmas Day.

Even if you don't normally say Grace at meals, there should definitely be Grace at the Easter Sunday lunch:

"Bless us, O Lord, and these Thy gifts, which of Thy bounty we are about to receive. Through Christ Our Lord, Amen."

Roast Lamb—two dishes using New Zealand Lamb. Beswick Lamb

Prep. time: 15 mins. Serves: 8
Cooking time: 1½ kilo/3 lb loin of New Zealand Lamb boned
Cook together
450 g/1 lb garden peas
1 sprig mint
6 spring onions
50 ml/2 fl oz sherry
juice 1 orange
For the stuffing:
2 slices bacon, chopped

122

2 New Zealand Lamb's
Kidney, skinned, cored and chopped and cooked in:
50 g/2 oz butter
1 onion finely chopped
125 g/4ozs chopped
mushrooms
salt and pepper
5 ml/1 tsp tomato purée
50 g/2 oz fresh breadcrumbs

1. Prepare the stuffing. Spread inside the loin, roll and tie.
2. Roast at 180° C, 350° F, Gas 4 for 1¾ hours.
3. When the lamb is cooked, carve and arrange on the bed of peas.
4. Thicken lamb liquor and add sherry and orange juice to serve as sauce.

Minty Rolled Lamb

Prep. time: 10 mins. Serves: 3 – 4
Cooking time: 1½ hours
1 large boned breast of New Zealand Lamb
75g/3 oz fresh white breadcrumbs
concentrated mint sauce
a little beaten egg to mix
grate rind and juice of 1 lemon
salt and pepper
mint jelly

1. Season the boned breast of lamb. Mix together the breadcrumbs, mint sauce, lemon rind and juice, seasoning and enough egg to give a fairly stiff mixture.
2. Spread over the breast, roll and tie securely with string.
3. Roast 350° F, 180° C, Gas 4 for 1½ hours—spread with the mint jelly 5 minutes before serving.

Easter Pudding

A Mrs Rundell, writing in "A New System of Domestic Cookery" in 1835, quoted in Margaret Baker's *Folklore and Customs of Rural England,* gave the recipe for what sounds like a very rich Easter Pudding which it might be fun to try:

"Beat seven eggs, yolks and whites separately; add a pint of cream, near the same of spinach-juice, and a little tansey-juice gained by pounding in a stone-mortar, a quarter of a pound of Naples biscuit, sugar to taste, a glass of white wine, and some nutmeg. Set all in a saucepan, just to thicken, over the fire, then put it into a dish, lined with paste, to turn out, and bake it." By "paste" she means ordinary shortcrust pastry. I should think you would need two or even three modern-sized flan dishes to cope with the amounts of liquid she is envisaging.

Easter Teatime

With relations visiting for Easter, you can have the pleasure of a proper old-fashioned tea.

Easter Biscuits (my mother's recipe)

These smell heavenly when cooking, and are light and crunchy and spicy to eat. You could ice them and decorate them as you wish: cut them out with a rabbit-shaped cutter and then give them dabs of icing for eyes and a white bunny-tail, or perhaps cut them with a circular crinkle-edged cutter and stick small sugar eggs on brown icing in the middle to look like birds' nests. Or they are delicious simply eaten as they are—which is the way we usually enjoy them.

> 8 oz. self-raising flour
> 4 oz. margarine
> 4 oz. granulated sugar
> a pinch of salt
> level teaspoonful cinnamon
> 2 oz currants
> one egg (medium-sized)

Rub fat into flour. Add sugar, cinammon, and salt, and then the currants. Add egg to bind. At first, it feels as if the mixture won't stick together with the egg, but if you keep on working it with your hands, you will find that it will. Eventually it becomes pliable and you can roll it out very thinly and cut it out into biscuits: do this on a floured table-top or board. It should make between 40 and 50 biscuits. Bake at gas no. 4 (350 degrees) until golden-brown.

Easter Cake

The traditional Easter Cake is a Simnel Cake (see recipe for Mothering Sunday).

"Lifting"

A very old tradition which seems to have been forgotten but might be fun to bring back, is that of "lifting" at Easter-time. It means literally what it says: you lift people! It is said to have its origins in Our Lord rising from the tomb.

First the women of the family sit the men in a chair, one by one, and lift them up, and then the women get lifted by the men in just the same way.

You decorate a chair first, with white ribbons and flowers, and then you lead the person who is to be "lifted" towards it and sit him down with much ceremony. Then four of you, one at each corner, solemnly lift the chair as high as you can, and put it down again. Once your victim is safely down, he can claim kisses from all who have lifted him.

Anyone who is a coward and refuses to be lifted must pay the others a fine of five shillings (that's twenty-five pence).

Cheesecake

This a very traditional Easter dish, containing as it does many of the rich things that have been denied traditionally to us during Lent.

Crumb crust: 5 oz. crushed sweet biscuits; 2 oz. butter. Topping: 1 desertspoonful gelatine; 2 tablespoonfuls boiling water; 8 oz. cream cheese; 4 oz. sugar, one small can chilled evaporated milk, 2 dessertspoonfuls lemon juice.

Make the crumb crust by melting the butter, stirring the biscuit crumbs into it, and spreading it over the bottom of a flan-dish or caketin.

To make the topping: dissolve the gelatine into the boiling water. Cream together the cheese and sugar until smooth and fluffy. Add lemon juice and beat well. Add the gelatine and the milk. Pour this mixture on top of the biscuit-crumb crust and refrigerate for several hours. You can then top the cheesecake with strawberries and serve it with dollops of cream. Adding vanilla essence to the mixture makes it taste good, too. Or the cake could be sprinkled thickly on top with grated chocolate.

N.B. You make the biscuit-crumbs for the crust by putting the biscuits into a strong plastic bag and bashing it with a rolling pin.

Bring, all ye dear-bought nations bring
Your richest praises to your king
Alleluia! Alleluia!
That spotless Lamb, who more then due
Paid for his sheep, and those sheep you.
Alleluia, alleluia, alleluia, alleluia!

That guiltless Son, who bought your peace
And made his Father's anger cease
Then life and death together fought
Each to a strange extreme were brought.

Life died, but soon revived again
And even death by it was slain
Say, happy Magdalen, oh say
What didst thou see there by the way?

"I saw the tomb of my dear Lord
I saw Himself and Him adored
I saw the napkin and the sheet
That bound His head and wrapt His feet".

"I heard the angels witness be
Jesus is ris'n, He is not here,
Go, tell His followers they shall see
Thine and their hope in Galilee".

We, Lord, with faithful hearts and voices,
On this Thy rising day rejoice
O Thou, whose power o'er came the grave
By grace and love us sinners save.

(1) Wipo 11th C.
tr. Walter. Kirkham Blount.

Rogation Days and Ascension

When buttercups are golden
And daisies bright and gay
There comes a feast of Jesus
We call Ascension Day.

On Ascension Day we commemorate Our Lord's return to His Father in Heaven. He disappeared from sight before His Apostles, who were left gazing upwards. We reaffirm our belief in the fact that Our Lord is waiting for us now in Heaven every time we say the Creed together: "He ascended into Heaven, and is seated on the right hand of the Father."

Rogation Processions

The three days immediately before the Feast of the Ascension used to be called Rogation Days. The word comes from the Latin *Rogare*, meaning "to ask". They are days on which we ask for God's blessing on our crops, which having been planted a few weeks ago are now just beginning to sprout.

The custom started in Europe in the fifth century. In the year 470, there was a terrible time of plague, and there were also some minor earthquakes. The Archbishop of Vienna ordered that there be special prayers on Ascension Day or on the three days preceding it, begging for God's blessing on the crops and land. Thus the custom started of people walking in procession around their fields—it spread rapidly across Western Europe, and in the eighth century it was established in Britain.

In parts of Britain, the Rogation Days became known as "Gang Week" or "Gang Days", from the Anglo-Saxon word "Gang" meaning "to go". At this time the people *gang* about the parish, blessing each field as they passed it.

Not only the fields were blessed: in seaside districts people would also want to bless the harvest of the sea, and so the parish would troop down to the waterside and bless the water and the fishing-boats and pray for a good fishing season ahead.

Beating the Bounds

At the Reformation, processions were banned. But many people still held them, because old customs are hard to destroy and the Rogation processions about the countryside in the lovely spring weather were very popular. People wanted to bless their fields—they were aware that God was the provider of everything, and they wanted to dedicate their summer work to Him and show Him that they knew that His was the power that caused the seeds to grow and the crops to flourish.

The processions had also been useful in showing people their parish boundaries. These boundaries were now becoming even more important as administration was changing. So it was decided that people should go about the parish to "beat the bounds"—to show everyone, especially the younger members of the parish, where the boundaries lay.

At the boundary-marks of the parish—a tree, a pond, a big rock—the parson would stop to read the Gospel, and when this had been done, the boys of the parish were beaten with willow-wands, to help remind them of the boundary-point. Sometimes they were not only beaten, but were bumped about, pushed into a stream or turned upside-down over a fence or hedge.

Old place-names and field-names such as Gospel Oak and Paternoster Field commemorate the old Rogation Processions or their descendants, the Bound-Beating walks.

Sidlesham, in Sussex, still has a Rogation procession, as does Staplehurst in Kent.

In some places in Britain, the bounds are still beaten—although these days the boys of the parish, dressed in their choir-boy robes, are no longer the victims as of old. They carry willow-wands and use them to beat old landmarks with much ceremony instead. The bounds of the parish of the Tower of London are beaten in this way once every three years, and the parish of St. Clement Danes has a ceremony which, in order to pass every parish boundary, involves a river trip.

There are still places, too, where a Blessing of the Sea is held, dating back to the old Rogation Days.

Well-Dressing

In Derbyshire, wells are dressed at Ascensiontide. The most famous are at Tissington, Tideswell, Wirksworth, Buxton, Ashford and Eyam. The tradition dates back to the Black Death when, it is said, no one at Tissington died of the plague and this was attributed to the purity of the water-supply. There is also a link with a terrible drought that took place in 1615—many rivers and lakes ran dry, and cattle had to be walked as far as ten miles to Tissington where the faithful wells continued to give water.

The wells are dressed by having boarded frames placed over them, covered with damp soil. On these are worked a variety of beautiful designs, all with religious themes. To create the pictures, flowers, berries, leaves and moss are used—there is nothing made from any artificial fabric of any kind. A short service is held at each well, and it is solemnly blessed.

How to Celebrate the Feast of the Ascension

Why not hold your own procession and bless your own garden during Rogationtide? In a family where every child has his own tiny plot, it is fun to walk from the house, and visit each plot in turn, sprinkle it with holy water and say a little prayer. By now, the seeds planted on Good Friday should be showing with some tiny green shoots. At harvest-time, when the summer is over, we will be enjoying what has been grown and giving thanks to God for all His gifts. The Rogation procession should end with a picnic tea eaten out of doors among the newly-blessed flower-beds and lawns. A special Ascension Cake—perhaps a light fluffy sponge or a meringue-case filled with fruit and cream—would be fun.

If you haven't a garden, you can still bless the flower tubs and window-boxes. You can bless an allotment.

And why not make Ascension Day the day when you discover your own parish boundaries? With a map and a picnic lunch it could prove a fascinating exercise—there is bound to be a park or a recreation ground at some point where lunch can be eaten. Consultations with your parish priest and some debate over the best route to take could pave the way for a most unusual day: you could end up rediscovering your own home district!

In these days when some people seem to think you need a car for every small journey, it is good to rediscover the use of our legs. Leave the car in the garage, and beat the idea that fun can only be had via an expensive and lengthy trip. There is entertainment, pleasure, and much to learn right on our own doorstep. Children in particular, need to know their own area well—for safety's sake because of dark evenings, and also because familiarity with a particular place gives them a sense of belonging, of roots. We should feel a real attachment to the place where we live. And that evening at family prayers we could beg God's blessing on our town, on the local council and all the people who live and work in our area.

An Ascension Hymn

To be sung to the tune of "will ye no come back again"!

Verse: Jesus Christ is now away,
            Seated at His Father's side,
            Yet He will return one day,
            At the final Eastertide.

Chorus: He'll come back to Earth again,
            Though we'll never forecast when.
            Prepared forever must we be,
            For His new Epiphany.

(J. Alain Smith)

St George's Day—April 23

Anthony Cooney writes:

> *The Day of St George is a musty affair*
> *Which Russians and Greeks are permitted to share*

So wrote G.K. Chesterton, over fifty years ago, lamenting the absorption of England into the mere vulgarity of an Empire. Yet as recently as the late 1940s the BBC were still able to rise to a concert of English Music on St George's day. As England has drifted further from Christianity in the fifty years since Chesterton's lament, so, too, has devotion to St George withered. Many Christians today question what relevance St George (or any other devotion or piety for that matter) has for the *modern* world. As though this were in some way an unanswerable dismissal of our Patron Saint!

We might ask "What relevance did St George have for the world of the fourth century?" Which, as it happens, was the "modern world" for those who lived in it.

Galerius, deputy of the ageing Emperor Diocletian, had no hesitation in concluding that George had no relevance at all for the Pagan War of his day. If George, the former favourite of Diocletian and Tribune of the Imperial Guard, had been relevant to the world of Galerius, to its cruelty, its avarice and its decadence, he would have continued to live in wealth and comfort in his villa at Lydda.

St Ambrose, Bishop of Milan, says of George: "George, the most faithful soldier of Jesus Christ, when religion was by others concealed, alone adventured to confess the Name of God, whose heavenly grace infused such constancy into him, that he not only warned the tyrants, but was contemptuous of their tortures."

This provides a clue to the astonishing spread of devotion to St George, from the Euphrates' frontier to Hadrian's Wall, within a century of his martyrdom. What was so important about this martyr among so many others? From St Ambrose's words it is evident that for many Christians, those living in comfort, those holding public office, those receiving official pensions, conforming to the world by sprinkling a pinch of incense upon a lamp before the Emperor's image, was nothing to make a big production of—a necessary concession to the facts of life which God would understand. George "alone adventured to confess the name of God", and so stemmed the tide of apostasy. Traditionally he is said to have confessed the Name of Christ before Galerius by deliberate choice and after mature reflection. According to the account of his life attributed to his personal servant, Passicrates, George sold his possessions and distributed his wealth among the poor, before setting out to the Eastern capital of Nicomedia, a journey from which he did not expect to return. To his friends, urging him not to be hasty, but to wait in hope of better times, he merely said "Pray for my soul, and if you can recover my body bury it in my native Lydda".

George was judged obdurate in his refusal to sacrifice to the Genius of the Emperor and was beheaded on April 23, Good Friday of the year 304 AD. The date has ever since been celebrated as his birthday in Heaven. His friends recovered his body and buried it at Lydda, planting a rose bush on the grave.

What had this rich and favoured man achieved by his stubborn sacrifice of Imperial patronage, friendship, and life itself? Within a few years Diocletian was dead and Galerius, his evil genius, had been slain at the battle of the Milvain Bridge. Constantine proclaimed Christianity the Religion of the Empire and the persecution of Christians ceased. Constantine raised a church over the site of St George's martyrdom, and another over his grave at Lydda. It would not be an exaggeration to say that, in God's Providence, St George had saved the Church by his example, "when religion was by others concealed". Hence in the Eastern Church he is rightly hailed as "Captain of the Noble Army of Martyrs", and as "The Trophy Bearer". In the West he is called "Champion Knight of Christendom". He is universally regarded as Protector and Exemplar of Youth, as Model of Chastity, as Lord of Courtesy who comes to the aid of the hopeless.

In England a church was dedicated to him in Doncaster in the 6th century; he was included in the canon of the Mass long before the Norman Conquest, and a somewhat fanciful "life" was written in Anglo-Saxon, which made him an "Eorl" of the "Shire of Coventry". English devotion to him was greatly enhanced by the Crusades, and in 1222 AD a Synod at Oxford enacted that St George's Day be kept as a Holy Day. In 1330 Edward III declared him Patron of his new order of Chivalry—the Order of the Garter. In 1413 a Council held in London ordered that St George's Day be observed as a "Double of the First Class with Octave", James II, our last Catholic King, chose St George's Day as his Coronation Day in 1685, and English Catholics observed his Feast Day as a holy day of obligation until 1778. In the eighteenth century Pope Benedict IV declared St George to be Protector of England.

England, then, has no vague, semi-mythical figure as her Patron Saint, but rather one who is exemplar of all those virtues to which the English have aspired, however often they have fallen short of them: Child of Faith, Martyr for Truth, Help of the Hopeless, Champion of the Oppressed and Lord of Chivalry. Could we not all this year wear his rose on his Day, and pray for England?

The above article was written for the *Roman Chronicle* a small Christian weekly, in April 1983, by Anthony Cooney.

A St George's Day Dinner

I am giving here the recipe for a roast gammon joint which I thought had a very St George's Feast quality about it and which I discovered in a cookery book produced by British Bacon!

> *5 lbs gammon joint*
> *4 oz. dark soft brown sugar*
> *half a teaspoonful mustard powder*
> *5 tablespoons clear honey*
> *one tablespoon concentrated unsweetened orange juice*
> *cloves*
> *six small oranges*
> *twelve glacé cherries*

Soak the gammon in cold water overnight. Drain well and put into a large saucepan. Cover with fresh cold water and simmer for 2 hours. Cool in the cooking liquid, then drain well and remove the skin. With a sharp knife, score the fat into diamonds. Mix the sugar, mustard, honey and orange juice and spread over the fat. Insert a clove in the centre of each diamond. Put into a roasting tin. Cut the oranges in half crosswise without peeling and put a cherry in the centre of each. Place the oranges round the gammon. Bake for 45 minutes. Serve the oranges as a garnish for the gammon.

How to Set the Table

Use a white sheet as a tablecloth. Across it stretch two lengths of crimson ribbon to form a St George's Cross. The ends of the ribbon should be cut into inverted Vs—this looks neat and helps prevent fraying. The ribbon can, if liked, be pinned to the cloth—this keeps the arrangement looking nice all through the meal and it is quite easy to do it in such a way that the pins don't show. A red rose—you can now buy very attractive linen or silk ones at very little cost—should be placed at the centre of the cross. Use red candles.

How to Celebrate St George's Day

The invitations should specify that everyone must wear a red rose (although on one occasion we made an exception for a Yorkshireman who insisted on wearing a white one!) and come prepared to sing a song or recite a poem. This should be traditionally English.

A few song ideas to start you off:
"In Good King George's Golden Days"
"Polly Oliver"
"The Ruler of the Queen's Navee" or any other Gilbert and Sullivan
"Land of Hope and Glory"
The "Eton Boating Song"
Hilaire Belloc's "Cautionary Verses"
Poems by Kipling, Chesterton and A.A. Milne

Trifle for St George's Day

Trifle:
1 packet of sponge cakes
a little jam
sherry to taste
10 fl. oz. water

133

Split the sponge cakes and spread them with jam. Arrange them in a glass dish and soak them with the water and sherry (according to taste).

Many busy people today do not have the time to make real egg custard, but if you do it is well worth the extra effort. Here are the ingredients:

> *1 oz. flour*
> *1 oz. sugar*
> *¾ pint milk*
> *2 egg yolks*
> *1 egg white*
> *rind of ½ lemon*

First of all mix the flour with a little cold mild and simmer the remainder of the milk with the lemon rind. Pour the boiling milk over the blended flour, stirring well and then return the mixture to the heat, stirring all the time, and allow it to boil. Remove from the heat and add the sugar, and when cool enough, the eggs. Allow to cool slightly and pour the custard over the sponge base and leave to become quite cold.

Alternatively, you could make custard in the more usual way, with

> *1 packet custard powder*
> *1 pint milk*
> *2 egg yolks*
> *½ oz. sugar.*

Decoration:

> *Whipped cream*
> *glace cherries*

Cover the top in whipped cream and arrange the cherries on top. Do not add any other decoration: the theme for St George's Day is red and white. A wide velvet ribbon tied around the bowl looks attractive.

"For we are the people of England, and we have not spoken yet".

May

> *May is the month of Mary*
> *Bright is the sun above*
> *Bluebells all nod in chorus*
> *Joining our song of love.*

Celebrations for Maytime are very old indeed, and have often centred around a female figure: in the distant past a pagan goddess and for today's Christians, Mary the Mother of Christ.

In ancient Rome the goddess Flora was the goddess of Spring: ceremonies in her honour around the Empire celebrated the return of vegetation to the earth after the barren winter.

All sorts of traditions involving flowers became established in Europe, in particular the crowning of a young girl as "May Queen", with garlands of flowers gathered specially for the occasion. "Fetching in the May"—gathering the flowers for the garland and shrine—was a joyful community event especially for the young. Father Mark Elvins writes: "It is plain that the May Queen has thus continued in folklore as a modified form of the ancient Roman goddess Flora. In the Middle Ages the church felt obliged to give this harmless but obviously pagan custom a Christian guise. Where pre-Christian customs had become firmly established the Church would seek to introduce a Christian context and thus May developed a special religious flavour, although the devotions were of a popular rather than an official nature.

"By the thirteenth century, Christian May ceremonies had become well established and in the fourteenth century Blessed Henry Suso, a German Dominican friar, could write of 'fetching in the May', once for Christ and once for 'the tender flower and rosy Maid, the Mother of God. He also mentions in his autobiography the May custom of making a little chaplet (garland) of roses' to crown a statue of the Virgin Mary. The chaplet of roses was a love token well known in the Middle Ages. Indeed knight would be given the honour of crowning with this garland 'the Queen of the Tournament', a piece of colourful chivalry which readily lent itself to a popular international devotion to the Virgin Mary. It is from this association that the prayer beads came to be called rosary beads, and being described as a chaplet they were originally carved in the shape of roses." The French word for rosary is *chaplet* and in German it is *rosenkranz*—a rose crown.

Many places in Britain have May ceremonies: little girls become "May Queens" with courts and attendants and crowning ceremonies in local parks. One of the most famous of May events is the singing of a Latin carol from the top of Magdalen Tower in Oxford very early on the morning of May 1.

Good morning, Missus and Master
I wish you a happy day:

Please to smell my garland,
Because it's the first of May.
                    (From *A Little Book of Old Rhymes*)

May Day is now an official holiday in Britain—the holiday being on the Monday attached to the first weekend in May.

Christian May celebrations in England received a new boost from the activities of Fathers Gentili and Dominic Barberi in the last century. They brought with them from Italy the tradition of giving special honour to Mary throughout the month of May. This had been started at the end of the 18th century by Father Latonia of the Jesuit College in Rome. He was worried by the immorality among students there and saw devotion to the Virgin as a remedy. Subsequent Popes supported the tradition with various declarations and encouragements.

May Crowning

A crowning of a statue of Mary, and a procession in her honour were very popular in parishes in Britain and the USA in the 1950s and could easily be revived. By tradition, blue is Mary's colour. At my Surrey convent school the girls taking part in the crowning ceremonies— usually that year's First Communicants—wore white veils edged with blue. The crown was carried on a cushion by the youngest girl in the school, and placed on the head of the statue by the oldest.

In its simplest form, the May crowning involves putting a statue of Mary on a pedestal, singing some hymns, and placing a garland of flowers on her head. Other floral tributes are then laid at her feet, and the shrine is kept going all May with fresh flowers.

Bring flowers of the rarest
Bring blossoms the fairest
From garden and woodland
And hillside and dale;
Our full hearts are swelling
 our glad voices telling
The praise of the loveliest
 flower of the vale.

Chorus:
O Mary we crown thee with blossoms today
Queen of the Angels and Queen of the May,
O Mary we crown thee with blossoms today
Queen of the Angels and Queen of the May.

Sing gaily in chorus
The bright angels o'er us
Re-echo the song we
Begin upon earth.
Their harps are repeating
   the notes of our greeting
For Mary herself is
   the cause of our mirth.
Chorus.

Their lady they name thee
Their mistress proclaim thee
Oh, grant that thy children
On earth be as true
As long as the bowers
   are radiant with flowers
As long as the azure
   shall keep its bright hue.
Chorus.

The flower we call "May" is hawthorn blossom but it is only one of many flowers that bloom in this month. For a crowning ceremony, little girls wear their best dresses and garlands of flowers round their heads and carry posies or baskets of flowers. A boy carries the crown on a cushion to Mary's statue, and the oldest girl taking part does the actual crowning. The other children then troop up and stack their posies around the shrine.

Laying flowers before Mary's statue is deeply embedded in Christian tradition: some Catholic brides used to lay their wedding bouquets before a shrine of Mary after the wedding ceremony, and pray there for a blessing on their marriage.

A Maypole

Dancing around a maypole is a definitely pagan custom, though very picturesque. It symbolises an ancient fertility rite. The Puritans disliked it and tried to ban it: maypole dancing, banned in Cromwell's day, was brought back joyfully with the restoration of the monarchy. Many schools still do it today, and not just in rural areas: the youngsters at the infants school of which I was Chairman of the Governors for a while, on a council estate in the London suburbs, danced merrily and most expertly round a maypole in May and it was very picturesque and a joy to watch. A giant maypole used to be erected annually in London in Medieval times: the name of the Anglican church of St Andrew Undershaft commemorates it: it was under the shadow of the huge pole.

If you wanted to make a miniature maypole decoration as a table centrepiece just for fun, you could use a loo-roll centre, and standing it upright, fasten coloured ribbons to its top, letting them trail down on to the table, surrounded by a thick ring of flowers.

May and Flowers

May is a good month for learning about flowers. If you want to keep the flowers from this floral month to enjoy later when summer is over, you could try pressing them. Buttercups, clover, white campion, large fresh daises, dead-nettles, celandines, and all sorts of grasses are usually good for pressing. You pick the flowers and keep them in water while you spread two large sheets of blotting paper and stack up some heavy books (a set of encyclopaedias is excellent). Lay the flowers carefully on one sheet of blotting paper on top of a book, cover them with the other sheet, stack the rest of the books on top, and leave for at least a week. The longer they are left, the better. Mounted, pressed flowers make a lovely birthday or Easter card or Valentine, or they can be framed and hung up as pictures, in which case they should be kept away from direct sunlight or they will fade.

The Song of the May Fairy

My buds, they cluster small and green
The sunshine gaineth heat
Soon shall the hawthorn tree be clothed
As with a snowy sheet.
O magic sight, the hedge is white
My scene is very sweet,
And lo, where I am come indeed
The spring and summer meet.
(from *The Flowers Fairies of the Spring*)

May 31st—Feast of the Visitation

On March 25th, we celebrate the Feast of the Annunciation, the day on which Mary was told by an angel that she was to have a child. This child was Jesus Christ, the Saviour. We celebrate His birth nine months after the Annuciation, at Christmas, December 25th. But what did Mary do immediately after hearing the angel's message? She went with haste to see her cousin Elizabeth who, she had been told, was also with child and was in the sixth month of her pregnancy. The meeting between the two women has been called the Visitation—Mary visiting Elizabeth. We celebrate it on May 31st— after the Annunciation and before the birth of Elizabeth's child, John the Baptist, on June 24th. The Scriptural account of this visit of Mary to Elizabeth is very beautiful, and well worth . . . reading aloud on this day. It includes Elizabeth's testimony of faith to Mary "How have I deserved to be favoured with a visit from the mother of my Lord? As soon as the voice of thy greeting sounded in my ears, the child in my womb leapt for joy". And Mary's response in that great hymn of praise, the Magnificat. The relevant Scripture reading is Luke, chapter one, verses 39 to 55.

Carob cake—see the Birthday of St John, June 24th—might be an appropriate treat for today, with the significance of the carobs and their link to St John being explained.

It is right that the feast of the Visitation, honouring Mary's role in the incarnation, closes the month of May, traditionally devoted to honouring her. It is an opportunity to round off the month in style, perhaps by having some visitors to supper, since this is the Feast of the Visitation! The theme of visiting—especially women visiting one another—could go throughout the day; this is a good day for looking up an old friend, or arranging a coffee-and-cakes treat with some one who deserves it. And of course, any woman expecting a baby should be shown special honour today. It is significant that the infant St John greeted Christ, His saviour, while they were both still in the womb—a story with a message for us today, when the value of unborn life is not fully recognised.

Whitsun and Trinity Sunday

Pentecost—Whitsun

Come, O Holy Spirit,
Fill the hearts of your faithful
And kindle in them the fire of Your love.
Send forth Your Spirit, and we shall be created
And You shall renew the face of the earth.

Pentecost is the day when we commemorate the coming of the Holy Spirit to the Apostles—the Spirit that Christ had promised them before His Ascension back into Heaven.

The name comes from *pente,* the Greek for fifty—Pentecost is fifty days after Easter. Its other name, Whitsun, is English and refers to the white garments worn by those who had been baptised and confirmed on this day.

I found some very attractive ideas for Whitsun in a delightful and warmly recommended book, Festivals, Family and Food, by Diana Carey and Judy Large:

"Whit Sunday is the seventh after Easter, the Church day of Pentecost, recalling the manifestation of the Holy Spirit to the Apostles. By tradition the appearance of the white dove at Pentecost lends itself to the theme of a 'white' Sunday, as did the white gowns worn by newly baptised converts. In northern Europe the connotation is also a natural one, with the blooming of white May, Hawthorn and Lilac at this time. For children this can be a time to celebrate the blossoms, bringing a few into the home if possible, or finding white daisies to place on a saucer of water for the table or weave into chains. Have a cake with white icing for tea, perhaps with an icing dove nesting on it. One friend says that she and all the family try to wear something white, blouse, shirt or scarf, etc, and that they always have milk and coconut macaroons."

They give the following recipe for Modelling Icing:

1 egg white
1 rounded tablespoon liquid glucose
a little cornflower

20 oz 1 lb icing sugar
Few drops of colouring when needed

Mix the egg white and glucose together in a basin, gradually add enough icing sugar to form a stiff paste. Turn onto a surface sprinkled with cornflower and knead until smooth. Wrap in cling film and keep in a plastic bag to prevent from drying—it can keep up to six weeks in the fridge".

And when the days of the Pentecost were accomplished, they were all together in one place. And suddenly there came a sound from heaven, as of a mighty wind coming, and it filled the whole house where they were sitting. And there appeared to them parted tongues as it were of fire, and it sat upon every one of them. And they were all filled with the Holy Ghost, and they began to speak with diverse tongues, according as the Holy Ghost gave them to speak.

(Acts 2: 1–4).

Come, Holy Ghost, creator, come
From Thy bright Heavenly throne.
Come, take possession of our souls
And make them all thy own.

The Whitsun weekend used to be an official holiday weekend in Britain until very recently—but now we have the Spring Bank Holiday weekend instead, which sometimes coincides with Whitsun and sometimes doesn't. However, as "Spring Bank Holiday" sounds rather bureaucratic and formal, many people still refer to it as the "Whitsun weekend" even when it isn't. This makes for great confusion. I cannot see why the deliberate secularising of our public holidays has been foisted upon us, and I make a personal plea for a return to the old sensible arrangement, which always ensured that we got a holiday nicely spaced after Easter, instead of a jumble of holidays in a row which is what we get now. The old system was well grounded in history, and was designed to fit in with established cultural patterns and not with bureaucratic whims. (The May Day holiday, incidentally, adds further to the confusion).

The Gifts of the Holy Spirit

There are traditionally seven Gifts of the Holy Spirit. They are: Wisdom, Understanding, Counsel, Fortitude, Knowledge, Piety and the Fear of the Lord.

Children might like to learn about these at Pentecost. One idea is to write each one out on a silhouette of a dove, & have these hanging as a mobile over the lunch-table. The doves could be decorated and coloured any way the children wanted—a project for a wet afternoon leading up to Whitsun?

I once saw a group of children acting out a simple Pentecost play for an appreciative audience of parents and friends:

Twelve children stood around a table looking glum, while a narrator explained that they were the Apostles, gloomy because Our Lord had gone back to Heaven at the Ascension. Then (off stage) came the noise of a rushing wind (children going ooooh!, getting londer) and the narrator, reading from the Bible, told us that the Holy Spirit descended on everyone, appearing like flames of fire above their heads. The children waved their arms above their heads joyfully, extracting as they did so neat rings of wire to which were attached paper "flames", which they had cut and coloured earlier from cardboard. They put these rings of wire round their heads so that the "flames" stood up, a bit like a single feather on an Indian's head-band. Then they took the Gifts of the Holy Spirit from a box on the table and distributed them amongst us—pieces of paper on which the names of the Gifts had been written. They read them all aloud to us first: Wisdom, Understanding, Counsel, etc.

As they moved among us to distribute them, we all struck up a hymn to the Holy Spirit together.

(This was at a Family Day organised in 1991 in Ipswich by members of the National Association of Catholic Families)

Trinity Sunday

Glory be to the Father
and to the Son
and to the Holy Spirit
as it was in the beginning
is now
and ever shall be
world without end
Amen.

The first Sunday after Pentecost is Trinity Sunday. It's a peculiarly appropriate feast for modern times, because it was started in the days of the Arian heresy—the heresy which stated that Jesus Christ was essentially a very holy man, but not fully the Son of God. This is a heresy which has resurfaced again in our own day: you will

142

find many people saying that Jesus was a revolutionary, or a caring social welfare worker, or a community leader, and that His Death on the Cross was a statement against injustice or an example of martyrdom like that of so many other men and women who have been persecuted for their political convictions down the ages. It is a denial and a distortion of authentic Christian doctrine. Trinity Sunday cuts across the heresies and reminds us of the fundamental truth: that Jesus Christ is God, one of the Trinity with the Father and the Holy Spirit.

Trinity Sunday should be of special interest to Englishmen, because it was in our country that it was first observed as a special day. It was St Thomas à Becket (1118 to 1170), one of our most famous Archbishops of Canterbury, who obtained for England the privilege of having a special feast in honour of the Trinity on the Sunday immediately following Pentecost. Special hymns and responses in honour of the Trinity had already been composed and were in wide use long before that, and Bishop Stephen of Liege (903 to 920) had written an Office of the Holy Trinity that was being used in some places on the Sunday after Pentecost and in others on the last Sunday before Advent. But it was St Thomas who obtained for us the special feast in England, and later this was extended by Pope John XXII (who was Pope from 1316 to 1334) to the worldwide Church.

Try a Trinity Pineapple Cake. It's so called because you use three pineapple rings to make a symbol of the Trinity on the top of the cake.

Trinity Pineapple Cake

You will need:
4 oz. butter or margarine
4 oz. castor or granulated sugar
4 oz. self-raising flour
two beaten eggs
and for the filling:
3 oz. softened butter
5 oz. icing sugar
one tin of pineapple slices (NOT chunks)

Cream the butter and sugar together, add the eggs and then the flour. Divide the mixture into two and bake in two well-greased round cake tins for twenty minutes. Turn out and cool.

143

To make the filling, simply cream together the butter and icing sugar, then add some of the syrup from the tinned pineapple until the mixture is of the right consistency for spreading. Then take three of the pineapple rings and leave them on one side. Slice up the other rings into chunks and add them to the icing mixture. Sandwich the two halves of the sponge cake together with this. Now dredge the top of the cake generously with icing sugar and place the three pineapple rings on it in a Trinity symbol.

You can serve this cake with scoops of vanilla ice-cream or with dollops of thick whipped cream—or both if you like.

Firmly I believe and truly
God is three and God is one
And I next acknowledge duly
Manhood taken by the Son.

And I trust and hope most fully
In that manhood crucified
And each thought and deed unruly
Do to death as He has died.

Simply to His grace and wholly
Light and life and strength belong
And I love, supremely, solely,
Him the holy, Him the strong.

And I hold in veneration
For the love of Him alone
Holy Church as His creation
And her teachings as His
own.

Adoration aye be given
With and through the angelic host
To the God of earth and heaven
Father, Son and Holy Ghost.

(John Henry Newman)

St Alban—June 20

Until some relations went to live in St Albans, that beautiful Hertfordshire market town dominated by its abbey, I did not know anything about Britain's first martyr. Most people in our country today do not know about him, which is very sad because he occupies a unique place in our national history and in the history of the Church in Europe.

The name Alban simply means an ancient Briton. You still sometimes hear Britain referred to as "Alban's isle" and other nations who have—with good reason—distrusted us or our leaders have referred to our country sadly as "perfidious Albion".

The saint whom we call Alban lived in the days when Britain was part of the Roman Empire. Like so many other Britons he had become a cultured Romanised citizen who had a sense of belonging to an important civilisation. He served as an officer in the Roman army, and he lived in the city of Verulamium, in what we now call Hertfordshire. The Emperor at this time was Severus and the official religion of the Roman Empire was that of the ancient Roman gods. Worship of them was obligatory, and a social duty, but perhaps for the most part lacking in depth of real belief. New ideas, a sense of a new era dawning, were already finding their way about. It was by now the beginning of the second century after Christ's death and Resurrection, and there were Christians all over the Roman Empire. Certainly there were many in Britain. They had arrived—who knows exactly when? Some people still maintain that the first to arrive was Joseph of Arimathea—the very man who had helped to take the body of Our Lord down from the Cross and who had provided a tomb for Him.

Concerned about the growing strength of Christianity and the threat it posed, as he saw it, to the unity and power of the Roman Empire, the Emperor launched a great persecution against Christians.

We are not sure of exactly what happened, but tradition says that Alban, who was not a Christian, was awoken one night by the sound of a chase outside his door, and opening it he saw a figure there to whom instinctively he gave shelter. It turned out to be a priest, fleeing from his persecutors. Alban gave him shelter for the night, and was so impressed with the man's courage and what he told him of Christ and of the eternal life that He had won for mankind that he wanted to become a Christian, too. They sat up all night, Alban denying the priest sleep because he wanted to hear more and more about Our Lord. As the dawn came they heard the pursuers once more. Alban by now had made up his mind. The ancient pagan gods of the British or of the Romans were an empty sham—he had come across the logical truth and could see no evading it. He begged the priest to baptise him, renouncing all the evil he had ever committed and all the false gods he had ever worshipped. Then he saw a way of giving the priest a chance to get away. They swapped clothes and the priest hurried down the street in the guise of an imperial soldier while Alban wore his humble cloak and tunic. When the pursuers arrived Alban greeted them and was arrested. He was not afraid and when he went before the Roman governor he refused to deny his newfound Christian faith even when given the chance to do so. He went on refusing through imprisonment and the threat of death.

145

Eventually he was taken out to the hill outside the town and there, before a large crowd, beheaded. (As he was a Roman citizen like St Paul, he was killed by the sword and not by the more painful and prolonged crucifixion).

Roman executions were always on the high land outside the town—think of Calvary. When Alban stood before the crowd his demeanour and the brief speech he had made so impressed everyone that they too wanted to find out about Christ. It is even said that where his head fell and his blood spilled on the ground a spring which was later found to flow with healing water, appeared.

At all events, Alban's fame spread. He was the first British martyr. The date was June, AD 209. When, many years later, the persecutions ceased and Christianity became the official religion of the Roman Empire, there was much devotion to him.

Much later a church was built on the site of his martyrdom, and later still an abbey. It stands today: some of its bricks are Roman, brought by the Saxons from the ruins of Verulamium. At the centre of the Abbey stood St Alban's shrine. This shrine, containing his relics, was destroyed at the Reformation, but painstakingly put together again in the 19th century. The Abbey is now an Anglican Cathedral. It is well worth a visit. Canon William Purcell, writing in *Pilgrim's England* (1981), says:

"The building to be seen there now is by no means the first on the site. Churches erected to honour a saint or other notable Christian figure or event often had humble beginnings. So at St Albans there would most likely be at first a small wooden structure. It was Offa, King of Mercia, who in 793 is said to have vowed to found a monastery on the site after a dream in which were miraculously revealed to him the relics of the Saint. Such an account needs to be treated with caution, having been largely composed by Matthew Paris, a mediaeval historian notable more for imagination than accuracy. Not a great deal is known about the Saxon monastery at St Albans: by comparison with its great Norman successor it was probably quite a primitive place. But it was sacked by the Danes around 870. A church dedicated to St Alban at Odense in Denmark indicates, furthermore, that these fearsome raiders carried off his bones, among much other loot, though there are elaborate legends about how they were tricked into taking substitutes while the real ones were for a time kept at Ely.

Verulamium, the Roman *municipium* at the foot of the hill, had long fallen into ruins. The savage invaders who overran the country gradually after the Roman withdrawal, had a superstitious fear of the massive buildings they had left behind, supposing them to have been the work of giants. They certainly never lived among them, preferring to keep their distance, using them, when necessary, as convenient stone quarries. This happened at St Albans, whose Saxon abbots also exerted their authority in routing out the brigands and other undesirables who were using the ruins of Verulamium as sinister hiding-places.

Thus, where Alban had once known the life of a Roman gentleman, and walked in the forum, and along the straight streets of an ordered civilisation, barbarism had taken over, just as might happen after a nuclear strike nowadays. The survivor was the faith to which he had so notably contributed.

The great days of St Alban's Abbey really began with the coming of the Normans. Lanfranc, Archbishop of Canterbury, in the course of his vigorous reconstituting of the English monastic houses, in 1107 appointed his cousin, Paul de Caen, as abbot. Under his drive the old Saxon buildings, by that time in a bad state, were largely demolished, so that once again the ruins of Verulamium were pillaged for stone and Roman brick and the beginnings of the great building we see today were made. Life changed also for the monks. The rule of St Benedict was firmly enforced. In 1115 the Norman abbey was consecrated, it had a scriptorium, or library and book-copying centre among the most notable in the whole country. It also had wealth, from lands and bequests: it had convents or cells—in other words, satellite houses—in places as distant as Tynemouth, Wallingford, Wymondham in Norfolk and elsewhere. It had also a monastic school, metamorphosed over many centuries into the St Albans School of today which occupies, among much else, the fourteenth-century gatehouse, the sole remaining part of the once very extensive monastic building.

The site of the old Roman city of Verulamium can still be seen on the open parkland beyond today's city of St Albans. The Abbey stands on the hill, and the town, with its colourful streetmarket and some lovely old gabled buildings, is spread out beneath it. I was godmother to a small nephew in a lovely ceremony in the Catholic church there which is dedicated to St Alban and St Stephen—Britain's first martyr and the whole Church's first martyr.

Tradition has given the name "Amphibalus" to the priest whose life Alban saved.

There are of course ceremonies in St Albans on St Alban's Day.

147

Some people believe he merits more attention in Britain as a whole. Certainly our children should be taught about him. The dramatic circumstances of his conversion would make a splendid subject for a play or mime by the younger members of the family on his feast day.

St Alban's Hymn

(Tune, Mirfield Book, 16)
ENGLAND! by thine own Saint Alban,
 Put thy Christian heart to school:
Learn to sacrifice and suffer
 By thy Proto-Martyr's rule.
Life in Christ is stern and selfless,
 Gentle though it be and bright;
Life in Christ is dying with him,
 Though in sweet and living light.
(from the hymn-book of St Alban's church, Romford, Essex).

Midsummer Day June 24

St John the Baptist's Birthday

I know a bank whereon the wild thyme blows,
Where oxslips and the nodding violet grows
Quite over-canopied with luscious woodbine,
With sweet musk-roses, and with eglantine:
There sleeps Titania some time of the night,
Lull'd in these flowers with dances and delight;
And there the snake throws her enamell'd skin,
Weed wide enough to wrap a fairy in.
(From A Midsummer Night's Dream.)

From the very earliest times men have celebrated Midsummer. It's a magic time of year, the time when darkness seems almost banished, when it goes on being daytime for so many hours out of the twenty-four that it seems absurd to try to go to sleep at all.

Midsummer is the time for merriment, and deserves to be celebrated. Our ancestors celebrated it in style, and even today most people have a sense of celebrating summer when they hold fetes and garden parties and barbeques.

One clear voice from English culture and history speaks to us of

148

midsummer's magic: Shakespeare with his immortal *A Midsummer Night's Dream*. Now there is more in this play than meets the eye. Of course it is all about young love, and love-potions, and fairies, which is entirely right for a midsummer fantasy.

But what about the significance of the ass's head? Do you know why an ass's head should appear in a midsummer play?

June 24 is celebrated by the Church as the birthday of St John the Baptist. The feast-days of most saints, of course, are not celebrated on their birthdays. A saint's feast is almost invariably the day on which he died and went to Heaven. But two people who were particularly close to Our Lord during his lifetime here on earth have their actual birthdays celebrated: they are Mary, His Mother, and St John the Baptist, who greeted Him while they were both still babies in the womb.

Why was Midsummer Day chosen, all those centuries ago, by the Church as his birthday?

The clue lies with Christmas. The Church decided to celebrate the birth of the Saviour on or around the winter solstice, which is why we have it on December 25. And at one time the birthday of St John was celebrated in January, to emphasise his nearness to Our Lord. But it was realised that it would be far more accurate to have it on June 24. Why? Because at the Annunciation (which we celebrated, you remember, on March 25) the Angel Gabriel told Mary that her cousin Elizabeth was also to have a baby and was "now in her sixth month". So St John the Baptist, Elizabeth's child, was born three months after that announcement—which brings us to June and Midsummer Day. So the date was fixed—and in medieval England St John the Baptist's birthday on June 24 was sometimes called the "summer Christmas".

This is where the ass's head comes in. An ass, of course, is always a major feature of any Christmas play or pageant. Mary rode on a donkey into Bethlehem, and Joseph put her and the Baby on the donkey again for the flight into Egypt. You rarely see a Nativity scene without an ass in a corner of the stable.

When the Feast of St John was moved to Midsummer, a few stray bits of Christmassy tradition and folklore went with it. That is why in some old Midsummer festivities you will see a man with an ass's head appearing, and it is also why Bottom the Weaver ends up wearing an ass's head in the *Dream*.

There is another reason why midsummer is linked with St John. He said of Our Lord: "He must increase, and I must decrease".

After midsummer, the days start getting shorter again—after Christmas they start getting longer.

How to Celebrate St John the Baptist's Birthday

Midsummer Day should mean a picnic—in the garden or in a local park. Play some Christmassy games, only out of doors—charades, miming, guessing games. With small children, play dancing and singing games:

"The farmer's in the dell, the farmer's in the dell
Eee, eye, diddly-eye
The farmer's in the dell.
The farmer wants a wife, the farmer wants a
wife
Eee, eye, diddly-eye
The farmer wants a wife.
The wife wants a child . . .
The child wants a dog . . .
The dog wants a bone . . .
We all pat the dog . . .

It's easy to play this game. All stand in a circle, with one as the "farmer" in the middle of it. In the second verse, the farmer chooses a "wife" from one of those in the circle, and forms his own little circle within the ring with her, dancing round in the opposite direction from the main ring. Then the wife chooses a child, and the child a dog, and so on. In the last verse, everyone pats the dog—who, however, has the consolation of being "farmer" when the song starts again.

To chose who shall be "farmer" first time around or who shall be "it" in a chasing game, or the first seeker in Hide-and-Seek, you "dip". Everyone stands in a circle, and you count round them, saying: "Ip, dip, tom tit. You are not it." The last person then falls out. The last one left in is the chosen one.

I met a Derbyshire lady in a train while I was writing this book, and she gave me an alternative "dipping" rhyme:

Ip dip dash
My blue sash
Sailing on the water
Like a cup and saucer
Out go you.

In our family, we always have ice-cream and ginger-beer on June 24, which also happens to be my father's birthday.

Ginger Beer

First make a Ginger Beer Plant:
Into a clean screw-topped jar put:

> *one oz. of dried yeast*
> *two cups of water*
> *two teaspoonsful of sugar*
> *two teaspoonsful of ground ginger*

Feed this every day for seven days with one teaspoonful of ground ginger and one of sugar. Keep it in a COOL place—or it will explode. Do not stir it.

Then, after a week, strain it through muslin and add:

> *the juice of of two lemons*
> *two pints of boiling water*
> *one pound of sugar.*

Make this up to one gallon with cold water. Stir, and then leave to stand for three hours. Then pour it into bottles with screw-tops. Leave these in a COOL place for a fortnight, and then the ginger beer will be ready to drink.

With the residue in the muslin: split it, and give half to a friend. Put each half in a clean, screw-topped jar, with 2 cups of water, 2 teaspoonsful of ginger, and two of sugar (do *not* add any new yeast—you don't need it) and begin again.

Summer Pudding

A very obvious dish to enjoy at Midsummer is Summer Pudding:
You will need (for six to eight people)

> *3 lbs of a mixture of raspberries, strawberries, blackberries and redcurrants, well washed and with all the stalks, etc. removed*
> *2 sticks of rhubarb*
> *9 oz. castor or granulated sugar*
> *10 to 12 slices of bread*

Line a pudding basin with bread: first cut a small circle to cover the base of the basin only, then cut fingers of bread, and line the basin with these—they should touch at the base, but leave the space of a fingers width between them as they bend up the sides of the basin (the juices from the fruit in the pudding will cause them to swell during the pressing so that they almost join when the pudding is turned out, they will create an attractive pattern like a crown). Stand the basin in a larger dish. Then take two sticks of rhubarb, wash them and chop into half inch chunks. Place in a saucepan with no water, but cover them with sugar. Cook until they have collapsed. Take equal quantities of strawberries, raspberries, black currants and red currants—enough to fill the basin completely. A couple of tablespoons of bottled elderberries from last year give a wonderful flavour if they are to hand. Put the fruit in the saucepan with sugar to taste, and bring quickly to the boil. Do not cook any further, but straight away spoon the fruit carefully into the basin, so as not to disturb the bread lining. Pour over the juices until the basin is quite full. Add a layer of finely diced bread, and cover with a plate or saucer small enough to be able to sink down in the basin when pressed. Add several more saucers, and then weights— a couple of family size baked bean tins are jolly useful. Next day remove the saucers, if any of the bread has not managed to get saturated with juice on top of the pudding, pour over some of the liquid that will have overflowed during the pressing. Run a knife around the edge of the basin and turn out the pudding. Serve with a great deal of thick cream.

Midsummer Day is essentially a day of rejoicing: of thanking God for life and warmth, and for the gift of laughter. It is a day for having fun, an echo of Christmas in midsummer.

O God, who by the birth of Blessed John hast caused us to hold this day in honour; give unto Thy people the gift of spiritual joy, and guide the minds of all the faithful unto the way of eternal salvation. Through Our Lord Jesus Christ, Thy Son, who liveth and reigneth with Thee in the unity of the Holy Ghost, world without end. Amen.

"Rejoice in the Lord always, and again I say rejoice".

Carob Cake

Locusts, as eaten by St John the Baptist, have traditionally been identified with the carob plant which grows in Israel, because of the shape of the carob pod.

152

Carob makes a very attractive alternative to chocolate cakes. I was given this recipe by a parent at St Philip's school, Kensington.

Grease and flour two deep 7" tins—Not loose bottomed as this is a very runny mixture.
Sift together:

> *7 oz. self raising flour (wholemeal is best)*
> *8 oz. natural soft brown sugar*
> *a pinch of salt*
> *2 teaspoons of carob powder (more if a stronger taste is needed)*
> *Rub in:*
> *4 oz. margarine*
> *Stir in:*
> *2 beaten eggs mixed with 5 tablespoons of evaporated milk and tablespoons of water*
> *½ teaspoon of vanilla essence—optional.*

Beat well
Pour equal amounts into tins and bake for 35 minutes at 325–350F; Gas 3–4; or 150C.
Butter icing can be used to fill and cover cake but add one teaspoon of carob powder if you wish a carob covered cake or,
Carob Icing:

> *melt 2 oz. margarine*
> *mix together 8 oz. sifted icing sugar and ½ teaspoon of carob powder.*

Stir this into the margarine with 3 tablespoons of scalded milk. Beat until thick and put a layer between the cakes and ice the top with the remainder and the sides also!

Ideas for Midsummer

Midsummer has long been associated with fairies and light-hearted fantasies. In Scandinavia, it is widely celebrated as a public festival, with dancing on Midsummer Eve, generally round a pole similar to a maypole. Midsummer has a special quality in countries where the sun only sets for a few hours in the southern areas and not at all in the north. Families decorate their homes with flowers and leafy branches, put up their own miniature maypole in the garden similarly decorated, and allow their children to stay up all night.

On Midsummer Eve, one tradition says that unmarried girls in search of a husband should pick a bouquet of seven different varieties of flowers from seven different meadows or ditches, and then sleep with it under the pillow—the bridegroom will then be revealed in a dream! Dew collected on Midsummer night is said to cure poor complexions.

Bonfires are associated with St John's Day. Sometimes the ashes are said to have special powers: in parts of Ireland they would be scattered over the fields to improve the soil. Elsewhere in Europe, it was a tradition for young couples in love to jump over the embers of the bonfire together.

Keeping a light on in the porch all night is another Midsummer tradition, as is hanging a bunch of flowers (some say it has to be cornflowers) on the front door.

Scandinavian dishes to try on this day include pickled herrings and boiled new potatoes sprinkled with dill.

Some Summer Saints

St Swithin's Day—July 15

Saint Swithin's Day, if thou dost rain,
For forty days it will remain:
Saint Swithin's Day, if thou be fair,
For forty days t'will rain no mair.

St Swithin lived in the ninth century, when England was divided into seven different kingdoms. He was a close friend and counsellor of the Saxon King of Wessex, King Egbert, and in the year 852 was made Bishop of Winchester.

A gentle and humble man, St Swithin made it clear that he wished, when he died, not to be buried inside the church but somewhere in the graveyard—ideally by the gate where people would walk over his grave. So when he died in 862 these wishes were remembered and a simple gravestone was erected where his body was laid to rest. For a hundred years people hurrying to Mass walked over the burial place of their bishop.

Then the local people started to talk about it: surely it was wrong that a man of such saintly life and such influence—a man who was honoured by the king and yet remained approachable and friendly to all—should have so humble a place of rest? It was felt that it was a scandal, and so a magnificent shrine was prepared for the body within the new Winchester Abbey, and plans were made for a ceremony in which the old grave would be opened up and the bones taken to the new shrine. The date was fixed: July 15th, 1964.

The day's ceremonies had scarcely got under way when a great torrent of rain poured down on everyone, sending the monks scampering for shelter. The ceremonies had to be postponed. The rain and stormy weather continued for a full forty days. And people began to nod to one another and say—just the way that people *would* say—"Ah, well, that's what you'd expect, isn't it? The holy Bishop didn't approve of people interfering with his wishes ..." Eventually, the removal did, however, take place and St Swithin's remains are still to this day in a magnificent shrine in a prominent place in Winchester Cathedral. The site of his original, outdoor grave is marked by a modern plaque.

Thus began the tradition that if it rains on St Swithin's Day it will go on doing so for forty days, and if it is sunny then forty days of sunshine will follow. Farmers and holidaymakers still follow the weather signs on July 15 with interest.

St Swithin is a sort of "home-made" saint: the official Church calendar doesn't list his feast-day. It might be fun to mark St Swithin's Day by keeping a weather record. Mark if it rains or not— and then note the weather for the next forty days to see whether the old tradition holds good.

Although rain at the time of year is not generally very popular, some farmers don't mind a light sprinkling: it is needed for the fruit trees. If it rains, they say that "St Swithin is christening the little apples". Rain will certainly help to make the apples fresh and juicy by the time they ripen in September.

St James' Day—July 25

As He was passing by, Jesus saw James, the son of Zebedee, and John his brother, and He called them both.

"Remember the grotto". July 25 is the feast of one of the Apostles, St James. Until the change to the Gregorian Calendar in 1752, this feast was celebrated on August 5, but in that year it was moved to July 25. However, children continued to build "grottoes" in honour of St James in August.

Why grottoes? St James, like all the other Apostles except for St. John, was eventually martyred for his faith. He met his death in the year 42 in Jerusalem at the hands of Herod Agrippa. His body was later brought to Spain and buried there. The journey was a difficult one by sea and so the symbol of the saint became a scallop shell. The place of his burial—Compostella in Spain—rapidly became a great centre of pilgrimage. Today the great shrine still stands and still attracts thousands of pilgrims every year. In the Middle Ages, many pilgrims went there from England. To raise money to help the poorer pilgrims, it became a tradition to build small grottoes of scallop shells—people would pay a penny, light the candle in the grotto, and say a prayer for the pilgrim. Scallop shells were carried by the pilgrims on their journey, too, as they were found on the coast in large numbers and were useful as drinking vessels.

As Father Mark Elvins has noted: "The old custom of children building grottoes of shells continued to be kept on the 5th August up until the Second World War and was seen as late as 1944 by a writer to *The Times* (24.4.44) when one was spotted under the arches of

156

Finsbury Park Station." Children would say "Remember the grotto" and people would give a penny and light the little candle which was placed on top. Grottoes were seen in the 1950's in Mitcham, when they were associated with the annual Summer Fair.

How to Build a Grotto

You could build a grotto in honour of St James on July 25. The traditional place to build one is on the corner of the street: if that is not suitable outside your own front door would do just as well. Collecting lots of different sorts of shells with which to make the grotto could be a traditional activity during a summer outing to the seaside. The grotto could be any design you like—perhaps using a box on which you stick the shells, or perhaps just laying them out in a square or circle. There should be a candle in a holder on top or in the middle. Inside the grotto there could be a holy picture or statue, some flowers in a pretty vase or jar, a Rosary, perhaps a miniature garden around an artificial lake made of a mirror. A woman who remembers making grottoes in Rotherhythe as a child recalls: "There would be sea shells forming a square enclosing a statue of the Virgin Mary with a jam jar of flowers, a Rosary, a picture of the King and Queen, of the armed forces and of film stars and actresses, with a nightlight". That was in the 1930's.

If children make a grotto and collect any money this way it should, in keeping with the proper tradition of St James' Feast, go to charity and *not* be kept! But perhaps, now that the needs of poor pilgrims are not so pressing and people fly to Spain for the holidays with ease, it might be nice just to make a grotto for people to enjoy and as a talking-point and not use it for fund-raising.

St Anne and St Joachim—July 26

St Anne, St Anne, she sits in the sun
As fair as a lily, as white as a swan.

St Anne's feast day is in the middle of the summer, in July, and that is why she is said to "sit in the sun". Some people think that the rhyme is "Queen Anne, Queen Anne", and that it refers to the English Queen Anne who ruled in the 17th century. But the rhyme is much older than that and refers to the saint for whom Catholics in pre-Reformation England had a great devotion.

St Anne and St Joachim are the names that Church tradition gives to the parents of Our Lady. Their names are not given in the Bible. But devotion to Mary's parents goes back a very long way in Christianity—St Anne being seen as the model of a good mother who trained her daughter in wisdom and in goodness. "Mary-Anne" or "Marian" was a very popular name for girls in medieval England, because it coupled together the names of Mary and her Mother.

The old rhyme could be used as a skipping rhyme on July 26—and don't forget to wish Happy Feast Day to any Annes you may meet!

Feasts of the Virgin Mary

The Feast of the Assumption—August 15

May today's venerable festivity, O Lord, bring us salutary aid, wherein God's Holy Mother underwent temporal death, yet could not be held down by the shackles of death, she who bore Your Son made flesh of her.
(Gregorian Sacramentary, 6th Century.)

Honouring Mary's Assumption into Heaven is something that dates back a long way in Christianity's history. You will find St Epipanius writing about it at the beginning of the 5th century, and St Augustine and St Jerome later in that century. St Gregory of Tours wrote in the 6th century: "The Lord had the most holy body [of the Virgin] taken into Heaven, where reunited with her soul, it now enjoys with the elect happiness without end ... Mary, the glorious Mother of Christ, was taken up to Heaven by the Lord, while the angelic choirs sang hymns of joy."

St John Damascene, writing in 749, stated: "St Juvenal, Bishop of Jerusalem, at the Council of Chalcedon (41D 451) made known to the Emperor Marcian and Pulcheria, who wished to possess the body of the Mother of God, that Mary died in the presence of the Apostles, but that her tomb, when opened at the request of St Thomas, was found empty: wherefrom the Apostles concluded that the body was taken up to heaven."

Mary's Dowry

Masses for the Feast of the Assumption have been written by many great composers. Scenes depicting the Assumption can be found in some of our most ancient churches and cathedrals.

In Medieval times, devotion to Mary was so strong in England that the country was known as "Mary's Dowry".

It seems likely that the title "Mary's Dowry" dates back to the 14th century when the young King Richard II gave thanks for the deliverance of the kingdom from civil strife after the meeting with Wat Tyler at Smithfield, and dedicated the country solemnly to Mary at Westminster, with a painting to commemorate this. It is interesting to note, incidentally, that the ancient chapel of Our Lady of Pew at Westminister Abbey, where the dedication took place, has a ceiling depicting the Assumption.

O holy and spotless Virgin, Mother of God, blessed for evermore, beyond compare, thou the most pleasing temple of God, sanctuary of the Holy Ghost, have pity and give ear to my unworthy prayer. Be to me, a sinner, a compassionate help in all things.
(Prayer of St Edmund, Archbishop of Canterbury)

And Mary said: My soul doth magnify the Lord,
And my spirit hath rejoiced in God my saviour.
Because he hath regarded the humility of his handmaid; for behold from
henceforth all generations shall call me blessed.
Because he that is mighty, hath done things to me; and holy is his name.
And his mercy is from generation to generation, to them that fear him.
He hath shewed might in his arm: he hath scattered the proud in the conceit
of their heart.
He hath put down the mighty from their seat, and hath exalted the humble.
He hath filled the hungry with good things: and the rich he hath sent empty away.
He hath received Israel his servant, being mindful of his mercy.
As he spoke to our fathers, to Abraham and to his seed for ever.
(Luke 1:46 – 55).

Our Lady's Birthday—September 8

September 8 has for many years been celebrated by the Church as the birthday of Mary. During the Middle Ages it was an important date in the calendar for many—it marked the end of the period of extra summer work that had to be done for the local lord of the manor under the feudal system (under the old calendar, of course, September 8 came a fortnight later in the season than it does now,

159

and so by the time it had come the harvesting was just over). It was a happy day when everyone relaxed and rested.

Find out about Flower Names

Devotion to Mary in England was so very strong in medieval times that it permeated the whole of people's culture. The names of flowers echoed it, and even of insects—that's how we get the name "ladybird". Kings invoked the intercession of Mary for the protection of the realm. Monasteries and abbeys up and down the land had statues of her and sung her praises. A feast like her birthday was the occasion for special prayers, litanies, and music—and fun and celebration

Fr. Mark Elvins in *Old Catholic England* gives the names of a number of wild flowers that are linked with Our Lady. It might be fun to get a book on flowers and go for a ramble and find out about them on her birthday—Our Lady's Thistle, Autumn Lady's Tresses. Our Lady's Bedstraw.

A Story from York

Recently I came across a strange and fascinating tale from York which it seems to me merits a place in a yearbook under the date of Our Lady's Birthday.

In 1975 an account came to light of an alleged apparition of Our Lady at York a hundred years before. The account was found among the old papers of a former prior of Mount St. Bernard's Cistercian Abbey at Coalville, Leicester. These papers included the report of a panel of nuns who had investigated an alleged appearance of the Virgin to three children at Castle Mills Bridge, York, on September 8,1875.

The *Yorkshire Evening Post in* 1975 under a big headline *'Miracle' in York—100 year old silence is broken* noted:

The vision was claimed by Joseph Hurtworth, aged 10, and his brothers Edwin, aged eight, and Basil, six, who, according to the nun's contemporary record, were the sons of "respectable tradespeople" with an uncle who was a Benedictine monk.

Parish records exist that the boys were baptised in St. Wilfrid's Church and, says Father Patrick Moynagh, they apparently lived at Petergate.

They saw their vision as they came home from visiting their grandmother, who lived near St. George's fields.

The date is the Feast of the Nativity of the Virgin.

The boys—who mentioned the vision to their family but made no public fuss about it and appeared almost to take it for granted—saw "a light behind the trees and at first thought it was a house on fire".

Then they saw a figure standing "pretty high in the sky and the water (the Foss) was all shining underneath."

The figure, with arms outstretched, was dressed "all in white and light around her, and a ring round her head with a few stars in it and the quarter of a moon under her feet".

She did not speak and the little boys told the panel that six or seven other people saw it. They said a man, passing with a woman, asked "What is it?"

I find this tale fascinating and would love to know more about it. A lady in York who has been helping me with research says there is no tradition associated with the vision there among the local Catholics, and the story is not well known. None of the children ever seem to have referred to it again.

Was it genuine? Or was it just perhaps some youngsters from a devout family, whose granny had been telling them September 8 was Our Lady's Birthday and who felt they saw something that echoed their own thoughts as they walked home together talking about Our Lady on a golden September evening?

There is to me in any case something attractive in the simplicity of the story and in the children's apparent belief that there was nothing particularly unusual about Mary coming down from Heaven to visit the world and hover in brightness over it on her Birthday.

Mary's Immaculate Conception

As we mark the Birthday of Mary on September 8th, so the Church, with complete logic, celebrates the feast of her Immaculate Conception on December 8th, i.e. nine months before the Birthday. (This is the same neat arrangement that gives us the Annunciation on March 25th, followed by Christmas nine months later). The Immaculate Conception—not to be confused with the Virgin Birth—honours the idea, affirmed by the church for centuries, that Mary from the very moment of her conception in the womb of her mother, was completely free from all sin—even the Original Sin that we all inherit from Adam.

161

Harvest Thanksgiving

Lammas (August 1) and Michaelmas (September 29)

We plough the fields and scatter
The good seed on the land
But is is fed and watered
By God's Almighty hand.
(*Matthias Claudius 1740–1815*)

To give thanks to God for the harvest is the most natural thing to do at the end of a good season. Our forefathers used to give the first ripe corn in August to the Church, to be used in making the Communion bread for a special Mass of Thanksgiving. This gave us the word "Lammas"—a mixture of "loaf" and "Mass". Lammas was on August 1 at the start of the harvest.

The end of the harvesting came in September and coincided with Michaelmas, the feast of the Archangel Michael. Saint Michael's feastday, September 29—now coupled with that of the other Archangels, Gabriel and Raphael—has always been celebrated in style. It is a day for a special thanksgiving for all the fruits of the land during the year.

St Michael was the angel God used to toss Satan out of Heaven. Lucifer, you remember, led the rebellion of the angels against God, and God had him and all his followers turned out of Heaven and into the underworld. Christians have always honoured Michael, the great Archangel, who did the actual job of turning Satan out. By tradition, Michael holds a flaming sword in his hand. He is there to defend the right against evil, and to be the defender of God's name and the protector of His Church.

Bottled Blackberries for Michaelmas

It is a tradition that blackberries are no good to eat after September 29th because "the Devil spat on them when he was cast out of Heaven into Hell on Michaelmas"! So the days just before Michaelmas are your last chance for picking and bottling blackberries and making blackberry jam. If you can't get proper

162

preserving jars, ordinary jam jars will do for bottling, with three or four layers of plastic—cut circles from plastic bags—held on tightly with strong elastic bands, in place of lids, topped with a couple of thicknesses of greaseproof paper. Bottle the fruit in a syrup made of ½ lb sugar to one pint of water, and make sure this syrup is boiling when you use it. Wash the fruit, pack it in the jars and heat it in the oven for half an hour, until it is bubbling and a slightly lighter colour. Pour in syrup and seal the jars. The blackberries will now be good to enjoy whenever you want, throughout the winter, in blackberry pie or blackberry crumble, or on their own, hot or cold, with ice cream.

Blackberry and Apple Pie

This is one of the most delicious of puddings. Allow two apples and a cupful of blackberries per person. Wash, peel, & chop the apples, mix with blackberries in a good-sized deep pie dish, & sprinkle very generously with sugar. Make a rich shortcrust pastry: 8 oz of flour and 4 oz each of butter and sugar, rubbed together until the mixture looks like breadcrumbs & then blended with water to form a pastry. Roll out & then cut it to the appropriate size to cover the top of the pie dish (the easiest way to do this is to stand the pie dish on the rolled-cut pastry & cut round it). Sprinkle the top with sugar before baking. Serve the pie hot with thick clotted cream or ice-cream.

P.S. It is fun to use the left-over ends of pastry to decorate the top of a pie. Leaves or plaited shapes are usual—or you could make a big M for St Michael, or spell out the date, Sept 29.

Roast Goose

The tradition on Michaelmas is to eat a roasted goose, stuffed with apples. The Michaelmas goose was fed on the gleanings from the harvest and so was plump and tasty. A number of places in England still have "goose fairs" at the end of September, although these days geese are not sold at them.

If you can't manage a roasted goose for supper on Michaelmas, you should certainly have a substitute like chicken, and it should be stuffed with chopped raw apple before cooking. Apple pie and cream should follow and there should be plenty of wine or beer. You could

163

put on the table anything the family has grown during the year: a pot of marigolds, some tomatoes, some mustard-and-cress; and before the meal you give thanks for all the food that people have grown for us this summer, on farms up and down the country. Why not sing a harvest thanksgiving hymn before the meal? The 19th-century favourite of which the first verse is given at the beginning of this section is widely known and still popular.

A Harvest Grace

Eat freshly-baked bread with the meal: some bakers shops sell special breads for the Harvest season, or you could even try your hand at baking your own—it's becoming increasingly popular and you can buy easy-to-use yeast and wholemeal flour in most supermarkets.

When you eat your harvest bread, why not use this special Harvest Thanksgiving prayer:

> Back of the bread is the flour
> Back of the flour is the mill
> Back of the mill is the wind and the rain
> And the Father's will.

The Meaning of Harvest Thanksgiving

It may be argued that harvest thanksgivings are out of date in these days of high technology and heavy industrialisation, when most people live in cities and have little if any contact with the land. One well-meaning cleric of my acquaintance even went so far as to devise a special "industrial thanksgiving" to replace the harvest one. This sort of thinking is very out-of-touch with the 1990s and belongs to the 1960s. There is a longing now among people for closer links with natural things. We are rejecting nylon and plastic in favour of wood and cotton and the "natural look". Camping and barbecues and do-it-yourself have never been so popular. At the beginning of the 1970s, an official report even declared that the old allotments—land leased out by local authorities in small plots so that people could grow their own vegetables—were out of date and had no realistic place in the future. Now there are queues for every allotment, and the demand is growing.

Michaelmas could be a time when we think seriously about how we are using the rich natural resources over which we have dominion. We could examine our own conciences in matters like dropping litter, and parking cars thoughtlessly at beauty-spots, and filling the air with noise from transitor radios.

It is also a time for us to pray for people who own and work on the land. Ruthless "factory farming", the demands of greed over need, the over use of artificial "fertilisers" which eventually destroy the soil, the creation of dust-bowls by the removal of hedgerows and trees to form giant fields—these are all ways in which modern short-sightedness and a lack of reverence for God's creation are spoiling once-beautiful countryside and causing tragedies for the future.

There is also the question of providing enough food for everyone in the world. Great tracts of land in some continents are still untouched, potentially richly fertile. Some of the worst famines in history have been man-made, and even today people go hungry because of corruption of officials, wastage, inefficiency and greed. Some of us waste food, eat too much, throw it away, or even let it rot, while others starve. What an abuse of God's gifts!.

An example of how human cruelty has the ability to destroy the fruits of the earth can be seen in recent history with the huge famines in the Ukraine in the 1930s. Ukraine was known as the "granary of Europe" because of its thriving farms producing and exporting grain. When it was taken over by the USSR. Stalin's Communist creed dictated that the small farmers were to be liquidated. Thousands were taken away to be used as slave labour on mines and canals in the East. Their farms were "collectivised" and confiscated from them, the food taken away in large vans and never seen again. The children and the elderly folk who remained starved slowly to death: some were shot attempting to conceal the tiny scraps of food that had remained, others simply died when the supplies ran out and they were reduced to eating tree bark, grass, and even soil. The country has never fully recovered.

Famine can also be caused by drought and other natural disasters: here we can give practical help and should do so generously. Michaelmas is an obvious time for making a family charitable donation to some group which is doing practical work to help the hungry.

Old Harvest-Time Beliefs

Myths associated with harvest-time show what a difference Christianity made to people haunted by belief in different gods.

At one time, pagans believed that the reaper who worked on the last sheaf in the field had to be slain: his blood would enrich the soil and ensure a good harvest for the next year. The gods were seen not as heavenly protectors but as objects of fear, to be placated with sacrifices. Hence the tradition of leaving the centre of the field to the last, with a couple of stooks standing upright in it: and also the figure of the "grim reaper" who symbolises death, and the End of the Year. Harvest-time is drawing towards the end of the year: the Celtic "Samhain", as we will see, fell in October at the year's end. We still have the tradition of a reaper with a scythe at our modern New Year's Eve: he used to represent the death of the slaughtered young farm-hand.

What a joy and peace—and what a revolutionary idea—Christianity must have been to our pagan ancestors! To learn of a Heavenly Father, who provides for all His children, who does not want to see any go hungry, and who sent His only Son to die once and for all to atone for mankind's sins—this must have seemed such a message of hope and joy to people who had lived by cruel and arbitrary savagery.

A Prayer to St Michael

We could end our Michaelmas meal by saying together the prayer to St Michael which is used to implore the Archangel's protection for us all:

> Holy Michael, archangel, defend us in the day of battle. Be thou our safeguard against the wickedness and snares of the devil. May God rebuke him, we humbly pray; and do thou, Prince of the Heavenly Host, thrust down into Hell Satan and all the wicked spirits who wander through the world for the ruin of souls.

Michaelmas Daisies

These bloom at this time of year—lovely tall purple daisies ideal to use in a posy for your Michaelmas table. I am told that girls at

London's Greycoat School are given cakes with purple daisies on them after a special church service on this day.

Guardian Angels – October 2nd

Today's feast is a very comforting one: it honours our Guardian Angels, the special angels that God has assigned to look after us. Angels are mentioned many times in Scripture, and Christians are assured that God uses them—among other tasks for our special protection and care. We each have an angel guarding us. This angel tries to protect us from sin—although we do not always listen to the voice of conscience which is the only way the angel can communicate with us! Sometimes saints have written about their guardian angels after being granted visions of them. Sometimes we may feel in life that we have been protected at a moment of great danger—perhaps from doing or saying something wrong or stupid or perhaps from real physical danger. Many of us will have been comforted in childhood by the idea of a protecting angel, keeping watch over us when it is dark or we are in a strange place or our parents are away or we are ill or lonely. Sometimes people have testified to a sense of a watching, guiding presence at times of real peril—an answer to prayer, a sense of peace.

Angels are part of God's created order. They are pure spirits. There are millions and millions of them. One day, we will meet our own Guardian Angels in Heaven.

Angel Whispers

> *3 oz. margarine or butter*
> *few drops vanilla essence*
> *3 oz. self-raising flour*
> *4 oz. castor sugar*
> *2 eggs*
> *1 oz. cornflour*

Cream the margarine or butter, sugar and vanilla essence until soft. Beat in the egg yolks. Sieve the flour and cornflour, fold in the egg yolk misture and finally fold in the stiffy beaten egg whites. Half fill small paper cake cases; (they stand better if you put them in patty-pans). Cook for 10–12 minutes in a hot oven (gas mark 6–7).

St Luke's Day—October 18

St Luke is famous as one of the four Gospel writers. He was a Greek, and tradition says that in writing his Gospel he obtained much of his information from the Virgin Mary. Certainly it is just possible that he met her when she was a very old lady: his Gospel seems to have been written about the year 70.

Luke is described in one of Paul's epistles as "my dear friend, Luke, the doctor" (Colossians 4:14). He travelled with Paul on several of his missionary journeys: one was a sailing from Troas to Samothrace and eventually to Phoenicia, and another from Phoenicia to Jerusalem. Later they went to Rome together.

For many years, St Luke has been regarded as the patron saint of doctors, and many medical organisations, hospitals, and doctors' groups will be having festivities in his honour around October 18th.

St Luke's Day is a good day for praying for doctors, and for all who have care of the sick.

We sometimes get a spell of warmer weather around St Luke's Day. This is known as "St Luke's little summer" and gave us the expression "luke-warm" for something that is neither warm nor cold.

An Old Prayer in Honour of the Four Evangelists

Matthew, Mark, Luke and John
Bless the bed that I lie on.
Four corners to my bed
Four Angels there be spread:
One to watch and one to pray
Two to hear my soul away
Matthew, Mark, Luke and John
Bless the bed that I lie on.

St Jude—October 28

It is an incontrovertible fact that in this irreligious age in Britain, our most prestigious newspapers do in fact carry every day a number of small announcements sent in by individuals who wish to make public their gratitude to St Jude for some favour received through his intercession. It has often intrigued me as to why the advertisement columns of newspapers are thought to be the correct—indeed the only—way of recording public thanks to this saint: surely a notice pinned on to a church bulletin-board, or even just a passing-on by word of mouth to friends, of the good news of a favour received, would be regarded by the good saint as sufficiently public gratitude? I think that an element of superstition enters in—people feel that in paying for an advertisement they are taking part in some chapter of a special ritual. At all events the results make interesting reading and probably do prompt more people to pray to St Jude as patron of "hopeless cases", asking for his intercession in their particular distress!

Just why this saint—about whom little is known—should be so readily identified with help in "hopeless cases" is not known. Perhaps it is linked with the fact that, as one of the Apostles, his name was similar to that of the traitor Judas and the latter even became better known than he. I feel that the injustice of this may have rankled with the early Christians—and rightly so—and he was given particular honour as intercessor in difficult cases to make up for it. Certainly as one living with the embarrassment of such confusion of names he would tend to be sympathetic towards anyone who brought an awkward problem to him.

As one of the Apostles, Jude was very close to Our Lord and in almost daily contact with Him, and like almost all the Apostles he eventually died a martyr's death, witnessing to the faith.

There are lots of different prayers to St Jude, and I am reproducing here one of the most popular ones. I got it from a thanks-advertisement in an American newspaper! You make a novena with it: i.e. you say it every day for nine days. After saying the prayer you say the Our Father three times devoutly, and the Hail Mary three times, and the Glory be to the Father three times. And you promise that if your request is granted you will publicise the fact and thus show your faith in the power of prayer over difficulties!

St Jude Novena

To St Jude, Holy St Jude, Apostle and Martyr, great in virtue and rich in miracles, near kinsman of Jesus Christ, faithful intercessor of all who invoke your special patronage in time of need. To you I have recourse from the depths of my heart and humbly beg to whom God has given such great power to come to my assistance. Help me in my present and urgent petition. In return I promise to make your name known and cause you to be invoked. St Jude, pray for us and all who invoke your aid. Amen.

Endless Cavalcade—A Diary of British Festivals and Customs, by Alexander Howard, notes that October 28 was "formerly one of the most important red letter days in the calendar of the City of London, where practically all the important events governing the affairs of the corporation are founded on the Calendar of the Church."

Mr Howard notes that until 1752 the Lord Mayor of the City took office on this day, switching to November 9 after the calendar change. It was also a day on which pilgrims went to Glastonbury to honour Joseph of Arimathea.

Hallowe'en, October 31 – All Saints, November 1 – All Souls, November 2

Hallowe'en is the eve of All Hallows, All Saints. Thus, Hallowe'en is on October 31, All Saints is the next day, November 1, and All Souls is the day after, November 2.

Bonfires—the word comes from the Norman French "bon feu" meaning a good fire—have been traditionally associated with Autumn since pre-Christian times. There was the idea of begging the sun not to desert people during the long winter months, of making fires as a protection and a pledge of spring to come. Father Mark Elvins notes: "Moreover, October 31 in the old Celtic calendar was New Year's Eve and the commemoration of the dead, when spirits were believed to walk abroad and the dead return to the earth. At this time all fires were extinguished, to be rekindled later from the many bonfires that were lit to welcome the returning spirits." The fire festival was known as *Samhain*, summer's end.

These traditions became so deeply rooted in local custom that the Church was forced to compromise by establishing in 837 the feast of All Saints on November 1, and the Commemoration of All Souls on November 2.

Only much later, in the 17th century with the "Gunpowder Plot" was a new element introduced. Recent historical researches would seem to indicate that poor Guy Fawkes was not quite the villain he was at one time made out to be, and he was almost certainly the victim of an elaborate series of plots and counter-plots. However, the celebrations of November 5 were vigorously promoted by the public authorities during the 17th century and have been part of the bonfire tradition for most people ever since.

However, up to the late 19th century, All Saints Day, November 1, was the traditional "Bonfire Day" and Alison Uttley, in a semi-autobiographical tale drawing on her own North Country rural childhood at the end of Queen Victoria's reign wrote:

"Bonfire day passed with the great roaring fire in the corner of the plough field, when potatoes were roasted under the stars and tiny Chinese crackers flew through the air.

Susan had never heard of Guy Fawkes, nor had Tom or Becky, or Joshua. It was a 'Bun Fire', when they ate parkin and treacle toffee,

171

and children danced round the fire before winter swept the fields.

As it died they leapt through the low flames and each had a wish. Then they stood in the fields to watch the other fires, on the hills in the distance, before they went in to their early bed."

Hallowe'en Ideas

It is fun to celebrate Hallowe'en—but only because we are linking it with the Christian reality of All Saints' and All Souls' which follow. The emphasis on ghosts and witches and eerie things-that-go-bump in the night is an attempt to return to old pagan ways. Christians know that old pagan superstitions and fear must give way to the joy of the Resurrection and the reality of eternal life.

Belief in various forms of fairly nasty "magic" is alas growing in the spiritual void of modern Britain, along with the thriving fascination with signs of the Zodiac and other silly forms of fortune-telling. The Catechism does well to warn us against "charms, omens, dreams and suchlike fooleries". As G.K. Chesterton pointed out, it is not true to say that when people cease believing in God, they will believe in nothing—in fact when they cease to believe in God they'll believe in *anything!*

Celebration of Hallowe'en should be linked with the fact that on the next day, All Hallows, November 1, we commemorate with joy the saints, men and women, who have gone to Heaven and are now rejoicing with God for ever.

Some people, indeed, say that the ghosts-and-souls theme of Hallowe'en is very appropriate for the eve of All Saints' Day—Satan is angry thinking about all those saints who slipped through his clutches.

A family commemoration of Hallowe'en can be a way of re-emphasising the Christian belief in life after death, and ushering in the month of November when we will be praying for the dead. But things should be kept on the level of family fun, with games and tasty food and a sense of drawing together in warmth on an Autumnal evening. Anything in the nature of seances and ouija-boards is definitely OUT. Christian families shouldn't be afraid to seize the opportunity if it crops up in conversation at this time of year of affirming their belief that Satan is real and that we do well to give a wide berth to anything that might give scope for his activities.

Children should be taught to make the Sign of the Cross and say

172

a quick prayer if they are ever frightened of anything "ghosty" at night or in a strange place, and they should be reminded that they were given over to God's loving care and protection at their Baptism and carry that seal on their souls. Many Christian parents rightly object to schools having celebrations featuring witches and even occult symbols at Hallowe'en.

A Pumpkin Lantern

The right thing to make at Hallowe'en is a lantern out of a turnip or pumpkin.

Pumpkins and Hallowe'en go together. In America, October is pumpkin time in a big way: I remember travelling through the New England states in 1976 and seeing the fat pumpkins standing on the wide farm porches, proudly lined up in order of size before the front door—and what whoppers some of them were.

You make a pumpkin lantern by slicing off the top (use a sharp kitchen knife or the dining-room carving knife. This is NOT a job for children, but for adults) and then scooping out all the flesh inside which, minus its seeds, you will use for pumpkin pie. Now cut a face—triangular eyes, a square nose and a long oblong or grinning mouth into one side of the pumpkin, slicing through the thick rind. Put a candle inside, and the lid back on top. A short fat candle is best and stands up firmly. The air coming in through the mouth, eyes, and nose keeps it alight. The lantern looks splendid and eerie sitting on the middle of the supper table with all the other lights turned out.

Pumpkin Pie

Start by making eight ounces of sweet shortcrust pastry, using butter instead of margarine or lard, and one ounce of brown sugar with the flour. Use this pastry to line a large-sized flan dish.
Filling:

> *one cup mixed dried fruit*
> *a good tablespoon brown sugar*
> *grated rind of one lemon*
> *one grated peeled apple*
> *sweet sherry*

two eggs
3 oz. brown sugar
good pinch salt
one cup evaporated milk or double cream
one teaspoon mixed spice
whipped cream and walnuts to decorate
2–3 cups mashed stewed pumpkin pulp

Put the first four ingredients into the pastry case, spreading them out across the bottom and sprinkling them generously with the sherry. Beat the eggs, mixed spice, remaining brown sugar and salt together, add the cream and the pumpkin pulp and warm it gently over the oven, stirring it all the time. Do not boil or even heat very much—it only needs to be *warmed*. Pour it over the fruit mixture and bake it in a moderate oven until it is set. Cool, and then decorate it lavishly with whipped cream and chopped walnuts. Keep it in the 'fridge and then serve it with a jug of more cream to pour over it.

Pumpkin Seeds

You can fry pumpkin seeds in oil, toss them in salt, and serve them as "nibbles" with drinks at Hallowe'en. I don't care for them very much myself, but some people find them delicious.

Soul Cakes

A soul cake, a soul cake, I pray thee, good mistress, a soul cake.

Going from house to house begging for "soul cakes" is part of the tradition of Hallowe'en that has crossed the Atlantic. Small Americans now go from house to house saying "Trick or Treat?"— if they don't get money or sweets or some other "treat" they play a trick on you. A proper Hallowe'en party, however, should start with the distribution of Soul Cakes to those who come begging for them. All your guests must beg for soul cakes. You tell them to say "A soul cake, a soul cake, I pray thee, good mistress, a soul cake", which is the old North Country refrain. You then give them each a soul cake in return for prayers for loved ones who have departed. Hallowe'en is a day for praying for all the people we want to meet in Heaven: departed grannies and grandpas and aunts and uncles and neighbours.

174

The Church's prayer for the dead is very beautiful and comforting and ought to be learned by heart by any child qualifying for a soul cake:

"Eternal rest grant unto them, O Lord
And let perpetual light shine upon them.
May they rest in peace
  Amen."

I can't, however, resist adding that my brother, when small, used to think it was "petrol light" which we begged to shine upon them!

Soul cakes are rich, round fruity buns. Use a rock cake recipe, but adding extra spices and fruit, and make sure the cakes are generously sprinkled with sugar before you put them in the oven.

Apple Bobbing

Apple-bobbing is the time-honoured Hallowe'en game. Put nice juicy apples into a bucket of water, and people must kneel down with their hands behind their backs and try to grab at them with their teeth.

Buns on a String

The same principle—but this time a rope is hung across the room (tie it to the backs of two tall chairs) and buns are hung from it (you thread each bun on a strong cotton with a needle, using the cotton doubled or quadrupled), and people must sit cross-legged on the floor and try to eat them without using their hands.

Chinese Whispers

The simple game of sitting in a circle, with the organiser whispering something to his neighbour, who whispers it to *his* neighbour, who whispers it to *his* neighbour ... the final version is invariably quite different from what was first said and it's very comic.

The Smelling Game

Different items in small cloth bags are hung from a rope, the same rope that you used for the buns. All the bags look identical. People have to sniff them and say what they contain. Ideas:

ginger
nutmeg
cheese
bacon
coffee (freshly ground)
tea
pepper
grated orange peel
grated lemon peel
lavender
rosemary

Kim's Game (for Older Children)

We did this in the Guides as a sort of memory-test. Put twenty different items on a tray, let people look at it for three minutes, then cover the tray and dish out paper and pencils and people have five minutes in which to list what they can remember: a watch, a bar of soap, a bun, a saucer, a tin of shoe polish, a bottle opener, a penknife, a brandy glass, a cotton reel, a prayer book, a match, a thimble, a can of beer, a drawing pin, a seaside sandcastle flag . . .

Blind Feeding

You need two cereal bowls full of broken biscuits, two spoons, two blindfolds and two willing adults.

Simply blindfold the two participants, sit them oposite one another, and make them try to feed each other. It's very, very funny to watch. A messier alternative to broken biscuits is bowls of cereal—but watch out for clothes, carpet, etc.

176

Parkin

This is a very traditional Hallowe'en and Bonfire Night food.

First, grease very thoroughly a large baking sheet, using softened butter. You will need a generous amount of butter: failure to grease the baking sheet properly will mean you can't get your parkin off it to eat!

Now take:

> *1 oz. butter*
> *2 oz. self-raising flour*
> *1½ oz. brown sugar*
> *2 oz. oatmeal or porridge oats*
> *¼ teaspoon ground ginger*
> *¼ teaspoon ground cinnamon*
> *2 oz. golden syrup*
> *a lightly beaten egg*
> *some split blanched almonds*

Put the flour, oatmeal, sugar, spices and butter into a mixing bowl and rub the fat into the dry ingredients until the mixture looks like fine breadcrumbs. Warm the syrup until it runs easily off a spoon. Allow it to cool slightly, and then add the egg to it. Pour this mixture on to the breadcrumb-mixture in the bowl. Beat very thoroughly with a spoon. Drop heaped tablespoonfuls of the dough about two inches apart on the baking sheet, and press an almond into the top of each one. Alternatively, put all the mixture onto the baking-sheet and place almonds at regular intervals. Bake for about ten minutes in a moderate oven until the parkin is firm to touch. Turn the cakes onto a tray to cool, or slice the parkin into slabs and turn these out to cool.

Another dish very traditional at this time of year is potatoes baked in their jackets and served piping hot with plenty of butter or with cream cheese. Some people wrap the potatoes in foil first, but this is completely unnecessary unless you are planning to bake them in a bonfire. Simply scrub the potatoes thoroughly, pierce them in a few places with a fork, and put them into the oven to bake. The crisp skins are the tastiest part of them: cooking them in foil just makes the skins nasty and soggy, and tiny scraps of foil lurk to set up agonising pain in teeth.

All Saints

For all the saints
    who from their labours rest,
Who thee, by faith
    before the world confest
Thy name, O Jesus,
    be for ever blest
Alleluia! Alleluia!

Thou wast their rock,
    their fortress, and their might;
Thou, Lord, their captain
    in the well-fought fight
Thou in the darkness drear
    their one true light.
Alleluia! Alleluia!

O may thy soldiers,
    faithful, true and bold
Fight as the saints who
    nobly fought of old
And win with them
    the victors' crown of gold
Alleluia! Alleluia!

All Saints Day is a Holyday of Obligation, a day when Catholics must attend Mass. It's joyful day, suitable for a special late-Autumn outing. How about a family walk through the park to enjoy the final glow of the Autumn leaves as they crunch and squish beneath our feet having departed from the trees in a glory of red and orange and gold reminiscent of the stained glass in church?

Children should know about their patron saints—if you don't celebrate the feast-days of various family saints as they come along in the calendar now is a good day for celebrating them all together. Tell the story of any saints whose names are borne in the family: you will probably find that you have a great variety. Children might enjoy acting out scenes from the lives of different saints. A little digging at the local library will provide information—it's amazing how much you can discover about even the most obscure saint!

All Souls

By contrast, All Souls Day is a solemn day, when we remember our duty of praying for the dead, and begging that we may all one day be saints in Heaven together. The right thing for adults to do is to

178

visit the graves of friends and relations today, to pray there and leave a little tribute of flowers. In some countries—notably Lithuania—processions are held around graveyards on this day, and people leave candles in small jars glowing on graves.

If you can't get near a relative's grave, visit a graveyard and pray for people who have no one to pray for them. And pray at home tonight, and every evening in November, for all who have died.

> Out of the depths have I cried to Thee, O Lord
> Lord, hear my voice
> Let thine ear be attentive to the voice of my supplication
> If thou, O Lord, shall observe iniquities,
> Lord, who shall endure it?
> For with Thee there is merciful forgiveness
> And by reason of Thy law, I have waited on Thee,
> O Lord
> My soul has relied on His word; my soul has hoped in the Lord.
> From the morning watch even until night, let Israel hope in the Lord.
> Because with the Lord there is mercy, and with
> Him plentiful redemption
> And He shall redeem Israel from all its iniquities.

Remembrance Day

They shall grow not old, as we who are left grow old
Age shall not weary them, nor the years condemn
At the going down of the sun, and in the morning we will remember
them.

It is surely appropriate that our annual national Remembrance Sunday in Britain—the day on which we commemorate those fallen in the wars of this century—happens to fall in the month of November, when the Church around the world is praying for the dead.

Remembrance Sunday is always the Sunday nearest to November 11th. This is because the Armistice which sealed the end of the First World War was signed at 11 a.m. on November 11, 1918—the eleventh hour of the eleventh day of the eleventh month. The First World War was a very terrible conflict which "put out the lights all over Europe", saw the deaths of hundreds of thousands of young men, toppled monarchies, ushered in the modern era. People in our country and in the old Commonwealth who had lost sons and husbands and friends wanted a national commemoration and mourning—and so the idea came about of observing two minutes' silence annually at the 11th hour on November 11. "Flanders poppies" were worn—replicas of those that bloomed on the terrible muddy Flanders battlefields in that war. The poppies came to symbolise a lost generation of Europe.

The Two Minutes Silence has become part of our national calendar, although now it is not observed on the 11th, but on the Sunday nearest to that date, and nor does traffic stop or radio programmes cease as used to happen in the past.

When we take part in remembrance services this Sunday, it should be to pray for the souls of those who died in the two world wars and the other conflicts of this century. When we wear a poppy it should be to remind us to pray for someone who has died in war.

It's a nice gesture to make sure that your local war memorial is kept clean and well-tidied. My father-in-law has given himself the job of caring for the one where he lives, and removing from its base the pepsi-cola cans and potato crisp bags and other junk. Who is looking after yours and ensuring that it is graffiti-free and treated with respect?

> *O valiant hearts, who to your glory came*
> *Through dust of conflict, and through battle flame*
> *Tranquil you lie, your knightly virtue proved*
> *Your memory hallowed in the land you loved.*

Autumn Saints

Martinmas—November 11

In November comes the feast of St Martin, the soldier who became a bishop. We often get a sudden spell of warm weather about the time of his feast-day, and this is known as "St Martin's Little Summer".

In former times, especially in the North of England and in Scotland, Martinmas was an occasion for a great feast, because it was the date when beasts were slaughtered so that the meat could be stored for the long winter months ahead. Whole oxen would be roasted and enjoyed, and there was much communal merriment.

St Martin is a most attractive saint. He ought to appeal especially to anyone in the Army,

St Martin

Martin was a native of Pannonia—in modern-day Hungary—and his father was very anxious that he should go into the Army. This was in the days of the Roman Empire, and to be an officer in the Imperial Army was a very fine opportunity for any young man.

As a junior officer, he was sent to Gaul—that wild land of North West Europe inhabited by the Frankish people who were for the most part pagan. There were some Christian cities where bishops were established and a Christian civilisation was beginning to emerge.

Martin was interested in Christianity and tried to find out about it. Its message attracted him, and he started to obey some of its precepts. He earned himself some notoriety by refusing to join in some of the bawdier songs and more outlandish activities of garrison life. He gave freely to the poor, was kind to his servants, and liked to pray. But he postponed the actual step of Christian baptism.

His first posting was to Rheims, and from there he was sent to Amiens. One bitterly cold night, as he was striding along in uniform having just inspected the sentries on guard-duty, a shivering beggar cried out to him for alms. Martin was warmly dressed in the standard issue thick purple-and-white cloak that was the hallmark of the Imperial officer. Looking at the beggar, Martin knew what he ought to do. He took off his warm cloak and, using his gleaming broadsword, sliced it in two. He gave half to the beggar and retained the other half so that he would still be in regulation uniform.

That night, the beggar appeared to Martin in a dream: but as a figure surrounded with shining glory—Christ Himself, still wearing the half of Martin's cloak. Our Lord reminded Martin of His words in the Gospels: "I was naked and you clothed me ... in as much as you did it to the least of these little ones, you did it to Me."

Martin got himself baptised as a Christian, and when his term of duty was up, he left the Army and decided to become a priest. He lived for many years the life of a hermit, and, attracting others to the rule of prayer and meditation which he followed, founded a small monastic community which grew steadily.

In due course his holiness led him to be chosen as Bishop of Tours, although he didn't want the job. As Bishop, his influence was immense—he won many from the Druid Religion to Christianity, and was a central figure in laying the foundations of Christian France. We honour him as St Martin of Tours, and if you ever go to Amiens you will see that the site of his encounter with the beggar is still marked today.

Martinmas Ideas

There could be a special supper for Martinmas with a hot casserole of beef to commemorate the old feasting traditions, served with hot baked in-their-jackets potatoes and butter.

Martinmas is an obvious day for some act of charity which will benefit the cold and poor this coming winter. It might be a good day for running a jumble sale ("give some clothes in honour of St Martin and his cloak!" could be your slogan!) or some other fund-raising event. There are still too many people in Europe who suffer from cold and deprivation in wintertime. Contact your nearest groups of Mother Teresa's Missionaries of Charity, or any other religious order engaged in this work, and find out what they need.

Making a blanket of knitted squares for charity use is a good, companionable way of working together to create something useful: why not start one on St Martin's day with a group of friends and resolve to finish it before the winter is out?

Ideas from Europe

In many parts of Europe, St Martin's Day is celebrated in style. In Sweden, roast goose is the traditional dish and goose banquets are served in homes and restaurants. The meal starts with a bowl of "svartsoppa", literally "black soup", made of goose blood and spices.

In Germany, goose is also a traditional feature of the day, and they say that this is because when St Martin was about to be chosen as Bishop of Tours, he tried to run away and hide in a flock of geese, because he felt he would be no good at being in charge of an important section of the church. But the geese cackled and the noise gave him away.

Other St Martin's Day traditions include the acting out of the meeting between the saint and the beggar to whom he gave half his cloak. This often forms an outdoor pageant with St Martin as a splendid figure dressed as a Roman soldier on a horse.

Lanterns

But undoubtedly the main festivity on St Martin's Day especially in France and Germany is that of making paper lanterns and carrying them in procession. Children form groups—either informally or as part of an official organisation with a band—and walk through the streets with paper lanterns that they have either made or bought. Shops produce a variety of lanterns depicting everything from spacemen to Mickey Mouse for the processions. Undoubtedly, it is as much a celebration of the arrival of winter, with its long dark evenings, as of St Martin. There are lantern songs and nonsense rhymes to accompany the processions.

Making a Paper Lantern

You will need a long strip of strong paper or cardboard, about 1ft wide by 2 foot long. Lay it out flat, and cut out some windows—star shapes look attractive. Decorate it any way you like. Now bend it round, glue the ends together and stand it upright. Draw round its base, then add a couple of inches round the circle and cut it out, sticking it in to make a floor. Attach a candle to this—the easiest sort to use is a "night-light" in a small metal container as this can simply be glued firmly to the base. The lantern will now need a long handle a string one like the handle on a bucket is best. This can then be hung over a stick—and the lantern is ready to be taken in procession.

Martinihörner (Martin's horns)

20 oz. flour
1½ oz. yeast
¼ pt milk
3 oz. butter
3 oz. sugar
1 egg
the grated peel of a lemon
2 tbsp. melted butter
1 egg yolk
sliced almonds.
Filling:
5 oz. sultanas and 5 oz. currant mixed with 5 oz. grated almonds or nuts and 5 oz. sugar.
For the icing:
6 oz. icing sugar mixed with 3 to 4 tbsp. hot water.

Prepare a dough from these ingredients. When this has risen, divide into 10 to 15 parts. Roll each of these out into a rectangle about 1½ cm. long. Brush this with butter, put in the filling, and roll together. Form this roll into a crescent shape, brush with egg yolk, sprinkle with sliced almonds, and let this rise again. Bake on a greased tray in a pre-heated oven, and then add the icing whilst still hot.

Heat: 200°C. Time: around 25 minutes.

Two players—one is called "Orange" and the other "Lemon"— stand opposite one another and join hands to form an arch and the others, one by one, troop underneath it as the song is sung. It is fun to sing the song with slightly different voices for each bell—with a deep voice for the Great Bell of Bow, who sings very slowly. The last two lines are not sung but said, and at a fairly rapid pace: Here-comes-a-chopper-to-chop-off-your-head". At the end the two who are making the arch repeat "Chop, chop, chop, *chop*" and at the last "chop" they bring down their arms on whoever happens to be underneath. He can choose to be either an "orange" or a "lemon" (it's kept secret which side is which) and goes to stand behind the appropriate player, his arms around that player's waist, as the song commences again. When the last child has been "chopped" and taken his place in one of the two queues, the game finishes with a tug-of-war.

The Oxford Dictionary of Nursery Rhymes suggests a grisly tradition behind this game, saying that it commemorates the days of public executions, when the condemned were led through the London streets to the tolling of bells! More cheerfully, children will enjoy discovering that all the places mentioned still exist: "St Martin's probably refers to St Martin's Lane in the City, where the moneylenders used to live; Old Bailey is near the Fleet Prison where debtors were sent; Shoreditch, where an old church once stood, is just outside the city walls; Stepney, nearby, is also without the city; Bow must be St Mary-le-Bow in Cheapside, whose bells told Dick Whittington to 'Turn again'. Which church peals 'oranges and lemons' is the subject of contention. Claims have been made for both St Clement's, Eastcheap, and St Clement Danes [in the Strand]. The former is situated near the Thomas Street wharves at the foot of London Bridge, where the berths for landing citrus fruit from the Mediterranean used to be situated. The latter, on behalf of which there has latterly been strenuous propaganda, and a special service held each March 31, is similarly placed. Sir Frank Lockwood in "Law and Lawyers in Pickwick" (1893) describes how in past times the tenants at Clement's Inn used to receive a toll for allowing the porters to carry oranges and lemons through to nearby Clare Market. The subject has, however, been given undue importance. In the second and fourth earliest versions of the song (c. 1760 and 1805) the 'oranges and lemons' couplet does not even appear."

St Edmund, King and Martyr: November 20

These days we think—if we think of patron saints at all—of St George as patron of England. But in fact that honour actually belongs to St Edmund, King and Martyr of East Anglia, who is commemorated in the ancient town of Bury St Edmunds. St George is the personal patron of the Sovereign, and is *protector* of the English realm, but St Edmund is England's *patron*.

St Edmund was born in 841, and is said to have been chosen as king of East Anglia while still not much more than a boy. He ruled over a Christian kingdom and when the non-Christian Danes invaded he took up arms against them. The Danish headquarters were at Thetford in Norfolk. Edmund was captured by them and subsequently killed, tradition says at Hoxne in Suffolk or possible Hellesdon. He was tied to a tree and shot at with arrows and then his head was chopped off. This was on November 20,869. He had been offered his life if he would share his kingdom with the pagan invaders but he refused. He was buried near the coast, where a town—St Edmund's Borough or Bury St Edmunds—grew up around the shrine. A monastery was built there in the 11th century.

St Clement's Day—November 23

Oranges and lemons
Say the bells of St Clement's
You owe me five farthings
Say the bells of St Martin's.
When will you pay me?
Say the bells of Old Bailey.
When I grow rich
Say the bells of Shoreditch.
When will that be?
Say the bells of Stepney.
I'm sure I don't know
Says the great bell at Bow.
Here-comes-a-candle-to-light-you-to-bed
Here-comes-a-chopper-to-chop-off-your-head.

Even though the rhyme was not originally linked with the saint. St Clement's Day is an obvious day on which to sing this well-known old nursery rhyme and to play the game that accompanies it. Young children will enjoy this. The music is easy: it is the same as the Westminster chime on a clock.

Who was Saint Clement?

St Clement was a Pope—the third Pope after St Peter. He is probably the Clement mentioned in the Epistle of St Paul to the Phillipians (iv. 3). He is most famous for the letter which he sent to the Christians at Corinth when they were dissenting against the leader of their church—this is the first known example of a Bishop of Rome making a direct intervention in a local church in this way. Clement was a deeply loved Pope and a great leader: the Corinthians found his letter so full of wisdom and concern that they used it regularly as a reading for meditation.

Legend says that St Clement was a martyr and met his death by being tied to an anchor and tossed into the sea.

In England long ago he was regarded as the patron of blacksmiths—presumably because they made anchors—and they used to fire gunpowder on their anvils in his honour on his feast-day. They also used to hold special Blacksmiths Feasts, all gathering together, with one of them dressed up as "Old Clem" and welcoming the others at the door of the inn.

Catterntide—St Catherine's Day—November 25

St Catherine was a very early Christian martyr—she is said to have come from a noble family and to have been very beautiful and highly educated. She protested to the emperor about the worship of idols and refused to deny her Christian faith to him when pressed to do so. She was offered her life if she would marry the pagan emperor, but she refused and was killed in a particularly cruel way by being broken on a spiked wheel.

Since few dates are given and there are no known relics of St Catherine, is seems likely that some of the information about her life and death is legendary. But she has given her name to many, many Catherines as the Christian centuries have passed, and some of these have become saints in their own right like Catherine of Sienna and Catherine Labouré.

Her symbol is a wheel, and the Catherine Wheel firework is named after her. It would be the right way to mark her feast-day by setting off Catherine Wheels tonight: there are plenty on sale, of course, at the beginning of November.

A Cattern Pie

You could also bake a "Cattern Pie". You make this by lining a round flan-dish with shortcrust pastry, filling it with mincemeat (see recipe on Advent Sunday), spooning some melted honey over the top and then sprinkling a generous layer of breadcrumbs over it. Then make some pastry "spokes" and place them on the top of the pie so that it looks like a wheel. It will need cooking in a moderate oven until the pastry and the breadcrumbs are golden and brown. Serve it with cream, and people don't get a slice, they get a *spoke* of Cattern Pie.

Margaret Baker notes in *Folklore and Customs of Rural England:*

"St Catherine was the patron saint of lacemakers and on Cattern Day until about 1890 when the lace trade declined, children of the Midland lace schools chose a queen and in white dresses walked the winter villages for money and cakes. As late as 1900 'wiggs', round spongy buns of fine flour with caraway seeds, were eaten at Wendover, Buckinghamshire, at Catterntide, with a drink of warm beer, rum, and eggs. Catherine wheels spun and sparkled for the saint, and in the evening the girls drew up their skirts to play the old country game of leap-candle, jumping back and forth for luck over a lighted lacemakers candle set upon the floor, to the rhyme:

'The tailor of Bister, he has but one eye
He cannot cut a pair of green galagskins
If he were to die.'"

She adds a footnote that the rhyme comes from an "oral report by Martha Chapman, 1910, collected by Mrs F.S. Chapman. Wright, Arthur R. and Lones, T.E. *British Calendar Customs: England*. 1940."

It is easy to see why the lacemakers had a holiday at this time of year, because they needed plenty of light for their work, and now the days were short and the dark nights long, they could give their eyes a rest and relax a bit. Perhaps St Catherine was chosen as their patron because she was a girl-saint with whom girl laceworkers could identify. Or perhaps the wheel (her symbol because she was martyred on a wheel) was seen as having a link with lacemakers' bobbins or with circular lace patterns. In Paris dressmaker girls had a holiday on her feast-day, dressed themselves in frilled mob-caps with yellow ribbons, and could collect a posy from every man they met!

Scotland's Saint:
Saint Andrew—November 30

Great St Andrew, friend of Jesus
Lover of His glorious Cross
Early by His voice effective
Called from ease to pain and loss,
Strong St Andrew, Simon's brother,
Who with haste fraternal flew
Fain with him to share the treasure
Which, at Jesus' lips, he drew.

Blest St Andrew, Jesus' herald,
True apostle, martyr bold

Who, by deeds his words confirming
Sealed with blood the truth he told.
Ne'er to king was crown so beauteous
Ne'er was prize to heart so dear
As to him the cross of Jesus
When its promised joys drew near.

Loved St Andrew, Scotland's patron
Watch thy land with heedful eye
Rally round the Cross of Jesus
All her storied chivalry!
To the Father, Son and Spirit,
Fount of Sanctity and love,
Give we glory, now and ever,
With the saints who reign above.

(Frederick Oakley, 1802-80)

On November 30 we celebrate the feast of St Andrew, patron of Scotland. He was, of course, one of the Apostles. He obeyed Christ's call to "Follow Me". A fisherman, like his brother Peter he became a fisher of men. He was martyred at Patras in Greece by being crucified on an X-shaped cross. This cross now forms the Scottish flag—a white X-shaped cross on a dark blue background. The cross unites with those of St George, St Patrick and St David to form the Union Jack—our national flag.

I invited an undergraduate at St Andrew's University in Scotland to contribute something on St Andrew for this book.

Stephen Holmes writes:

"According to legend St Rule (or Regulus), a Greek monk, was warned by a vision in the year 345 that the Emperor Constantine intended to remove the holy relics of the Apostle Andrew from Patras to his new capital of Constantinople. The saint thus took some relics from the shrine and, together with a company of devout men and women, sailed to 'a region towards the West, situate in the utmost part of the world'. On disembarking he is said to have built a church on the site that is now St Andrews. What basis of truth there is in this it is impossible to say, but another legend may shed some more light on the story. Here it is said that at the time when St Regulus landed, a vision of the Apostle Andrew was granted to Angus MacFergus, King of the Picts, promising him victory over his enemies. In gratitude for the subsequent victory, Angus dedicated the place to which the relics had been brought "to God and St Andrew, to be head and mother of all the churches in the kingdom

189

of the Picts." There was then a solemn procession around this place led by St Regulus carrying the holy relics.

"This association with Angus seems to point more to a foundation date in the middle of the eighth century, although a monastery was said to have been founded at Kilrymount (St Andrews) by St Cainnech, a companion of St Columba, late in the sixth century. Whatever the truth, by the ninth century there was a settlement of Celtic monks (called Culdees meaning 'friends of Good') and in 908 Scotland's only bishopric was transferred from Abernethy to St Andrews, in order to be near the holy relics."

St Andrew is usually depicted as a fisherman, wearing a simple tunic and sandals and hauling on his nets. Families could mark his feast by eating a fish supper tonight and saying a prayer to St Andrew as part of the grace before the meal.

We humbly beseech Thy Majesty, O Lord, that as Blessed Andrew the Apostle was raised up to be a preacher and ruler in Thy Church, so he may be our constant intercessor with Thee. Through Our Lord Jesus Christ, Thy Son, who lives and reigns with Thee in the unity of the Holy Ghost, world without end, Amen.

My Daily Prayer, U.S.A.

St Andrew's Day is a good day to try out some special Scottish foods. Try colcannon, petticoat tails shortbread, haggis, bannocks, Dundee cake, or baked haddock.

Colcannon (Serves 4-6)

6 well-scrubbed potatoes, quartered
one pound of chopped raw cabbage
2 oz. butter
⅜ pt. luke-warm milk
6 spring onions, including two inches of the tops.
Cut the spring onions lengthwise in half and then slice finely
teaspoon salt
some pepper
teaspoon chopped parsley

Boil the potatoes in salted water. Boil the cabbage until it is *just* cooked, and then drain very thoroughly. Then fry it gently in the butter, and set it aside. Drain the potatoes and mash them with a fork with 6 tablespoons of the milk. Stir in the cooked cabbage and the spring onions, add the salt and a little pepper, turn into a dish and sprinkle with parsley.

Shortbread for St Andrew's Day

175 g/6 oz butter
125 g/4½ oz sugar
250 g/9 oz plain flour
small quantity of cold milk (about 2 tablespoons)

Cream the butter & sugar together and then, using your hands, work in the flour. Add sufficient milk to make to a workable dough. Roll this out quite thin and cut it into any shapes you like using a pastry-cutter, or make one big circle & draw lines on it out from the centre so that the shortbread can be cut into triangles. Prick the dough all over with a fork when it is rolled out. Bake for 20 minutes at 170 degrees C or 325 F (Gas mark 3). Dredge with sugar and eat at tea-time or with morning coffee.

And with St Clement's Day and Catterntide and St Andrew's Day, and praying for the dead in November, we come slowly to the end of the Church's year. For, following ancient custom and instinct, the Church sees Autumn, when nature is dying around us for winter, as the year's end and beginning. The Church's year starts again with Advent: first one, and then two, and then more, candles are lit on the Advent Wreath, and Christ our Light enters into our lives as a tiny new-born baby. The world is made new again.

The Church's liturgy for Advent, in its choice of Scripture readings, points not only to the birth of Christ into the world at Christmas, but to His second coming at the end of time.

The feasts and festivals we celebrate on earth are but a foretaste of what Christians can expect in Heaven. We do not known when Jesus Christ will come again—we do know that in His kingdom in Paradise there will indeed be a Heavenly feast.

1. 1752
2. St Anne, mother of the Blessed Virgin Mary. She "sits in the sun," because her feast comes in the summer, on July 26.
3. January 6, Epiphany—the 12th and final day of Christmas festivities.
4. Gaudette. It means "rejoice."
5. October 31—the Eve of All Hallows, or All Saints, on November 1.
6. February 2. It commemorates the day Our Lord was presented as a baby in the Temple and it was prophesied that He would be "a light to all people." We light candles in His honour.
7. St Catherine's Day—November 23.
8. Building a "grotto" for St James' Day on July 25.
9. "Carnival" means "goodbye to meat," and traditional carnival time is just before Lent.
10. December 31 is the feast of St Sylvester.
11. It is the 50th day (Greek: pente, 50) after Easter.
12. "The Dowry of Mary."
13. June 24—Midsummer.
14. The Fifth Day.
15. St Swithin.
16. A specially decorated egg that you roll downhill at Easter.
17. The first Christian martyr, feast day December 26.
18. An Archbishop of Canterbury, martyred in the reign of Henry II. Feast day December 29.
19. To go to Confession and receive absolution.
20. The day before Shrove Tuesday—you eat up your "collops" of meat before Lent.
21. Rogationtide is the three days before Ascension. The traditional thing to do is to bless the growing crops.
22. Because Christ is the "paschal lamb,"—and because Easter is the Passover, when the Jews ate lamb roasted with herbs.
23. Maundy money is special money distributed by the Sovereign in England on Holy Thursday to poor men and women in an ancient custom commemorating our Lord's love and service towards His Apostles.
24. Spy Wednesday is the day before Maundy Thursday.

Answers to the Christmas Quiz

Hold this page up to a mirror!

Book of Feasts and Seasons

Bibliography

A Christmas Book—an anthology for moderns. D.B. Wyndham Lewis and G.C. Heseltine. J.M. Dent & Sons, 1928.

The Penguin Dictionary of Saints, *ed.* Donald Attwater, Penguin 1965.

Little House on the Prairie, by Laura Ingalls Wilder (Methuen, 1937) Penguin 1964.

The Best of British Bacon Recipes, by Mary Novak. The Sales Machine and British Bacon, 1979.

The Year and Our Children, by Mary Reed Newland, Longmans, Green & Co. 1956.

The Country Child, by Alison Uttley. Faber and Faber, 1931, Penguin 1963.

A Christmas Celebration. the Wanderer Press, 1983.

Festivals, Family and Food, by Diana Carey and Judy Large. Hawthorn Press, 1983.

The Oxford Dictionary of Nursery Rhymes, Iona and Peter Opie. Oxford University Press, 1952.

Virgin Wholly Marvellous—Praises of Mary by the Popes, Councils, Saints and Doctors of the Church, *ed.* Peter Brookby, Ravengate Press, Cambridge, Mass., USA.

Flower Fairies of the Spring, and Flower Fairies of the Summer, by Cicely M. Barker. Blackie & Sons Ltd.

Endless Cavalade—A Diary of British Festivals and Customs, by Alexander Howard. Arthur Baker Ltd., 1964.

The Foresight Wholefood Cookbook—for Building Healthy Families, by Norman and Ruth Jervis. Roberts Publications, 1984.

Hidden Art, by Edith Schaeffer. Tyndale House Publishers, Wheaton, Illinois, 1971.

Old Catholic England, by Fr. Mark Elvins. Catholic Truth Society.

The Modern Catholic Dictionary. John A. Harden S.J. Robert Hale, 1980.

A Little Book of Old Rhymes. Blackie & Sons Ltd.

Customs and Traditions of England, by Garry Hogg, David and Charles, 1979

Folklore and Customs of Rural England, by Margaret Baker. David and Charles, 1974.

The Divine Office—The Liturgy of the Hours According to the Roman Rite. Collins, 1974.

My Daily Prayer. Confraternity of the Precious Blood, U.S. A., 1955.

Really Easy but Delicious, by Pat Kennison and Dreda Tryon.

Celebration Hymnal. Mayhew-McCrimmon, 1977.

Saint George—Who Was He? Father Mark Elvins. Catholic Publishing Company, Ascot.

Easter and its Customs, Christina Hole, Richard Bell, 1961.

Pilgrim's England—A Personal Journey, William Purcell, Longman, 1981.

Contents

Contents